Praise for *The Price of Love*

We Africans know only too well that Islamism is a monstrous fanaticism that must be fought with force and determination — a reality that Sabatina James' personal history puts into sharp relief. *The Price of Love* is a gripping and, at times, graphic wake-up call to the West. It is urgent and utterly essential that this call is heard clearly and understood thoroughly before it is too late. We cannot afford to ignore it if future generations are to enjoy the God-given liberty upon which Western culture relies.

But this book is not only a warning — it is also a witness to the fact that "the Truth will set you free" (John 8:32). For, by encountering the saving Truth, the person of Jesus Christ, Sabatina James has been set free from even the worst of the persecutions directed against her. She knows that the price of that freedom is the Cross, which Christ has carried for us and which we must each embrace and carry in our turn. This is the price of true love, and it is one well worth paying, for it does truly set us free.

Robert Cardinal Sarah,
Prefect Emeritus
Congregation for Divine Worship and Discipline of the Sacraments

This is a personal story about one woman's brave exit from Islam and the dangers she has faced and is still facing from Muslims who regard conversion, especially to Christianity, as treasonous and worthy of death. But it is also an example of what tens of thousands of former Muslims experience, though their struggles and persecution are little known in the West. The "warning to the West" in the final chapter is an urgent appeal to recognize the nature of Islam, its militancy (even when it is not "extremist") toward those outside the faith, and the threat that large numbers of Islamic emigres now pose to Christian and formerly Christian nations. This book will open your eyes to realities that many of us almost willfully choose not to see.

Robert Royal,
Author, *The Martyrs of the New Millennium*

THE PRICE OF LOVE

SABATINA JAMES

THE PRICE OF *Love*

The Fate of a Woman —
and a Warning to the West

SOPHIA INSTITUTE PRESS
Manchester, New Hampshire

Sophia Institute Press
Box 5284, Manchester, NH 03108
1-800-888-9344
www.SophiaInstitute.com

Sophia Institute Press is a registered trademark of Sophia Institute.

paperback ISBN 979-8-88911-496-3

ebook ISBN 979-8-88911-497-0

Library of Congress Control Number: 2025942868

First printing

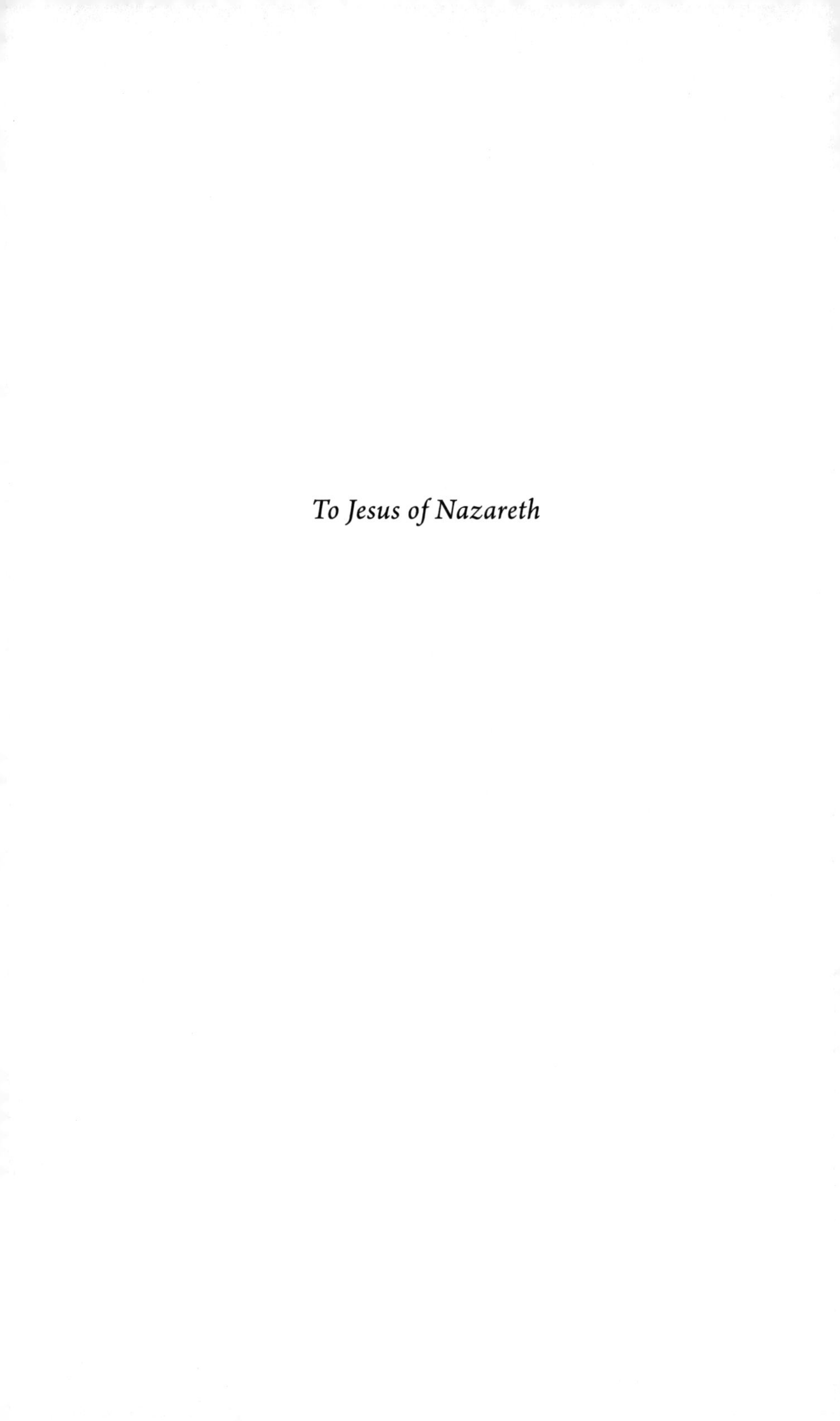

To Jesus of Nazareth

Contents

THE PRICE OF LOVE

Foreword

MANY YEARS HAVE passed since the night I was almost murdered. But sometimes, when I drive down the street and accidentally hit a speed bump too hard, the memories flood back, and I start to panic. My heart races: I feel like I've just driven over the person whose body on that night slammed against my car. Was it a man or a woman? I am not sure. It was dark and I was being chased by people who wanted to kill me.

Memories of my family — and of death hunting me down — occupy my mind, but I am reminded of God's promise in Psalm 91: "For he hath given his angels charge over thee; to keep thee in all thy ways" (v. 11). The God whose name I defended delivered me from my enemies.

Today, I am exiled from the land where my parents and my forebears were born. Divine Providence has brought me here to the Land of Liberty. I am surrounded by grand homes and fast cars, and as I recover my senses from the speed bump incident, the realization that I am forever torn away from the country of my birth gives me pain. But I cannot return. To return would mean a death sentence, if not by the government, then surely at the hands of a mob.

I have done nothing criminal. Nothing shameful. Still, I am afraid of the people I love most in the world and those who share their faith. My story is one of love, of belief, and of the conflicts that arise when you grow up in the West but are forced to live as if you were still in Pakistan.

In the West, religion may matter only once a week, or during the holidays, or as a rite of passage: in preparation for a First Communion, bar mitzvah, or maybe a wedding. But in general, it is distinct from the rest of daily life. It keeps quiet when you are at school or at work; it does not tell you how you must dress; it does not disrupt your social interactions or determine your career path. Religion is largely private, a matter of personal belief.

But in the world where I am from, religion is omnipresent. Allah exists in every word and every action; every hope, request, or opinion is prefaced by *inshallah*, "Allah willing." The days are lived in rhythm with the *azan*, the five daily calls to prayer. At dawn, the imam's voice rises over rooftops, carrying words that have echoed for centuries:

> Allah Hu Akbar!
> Ashhadu an la ilaha illa Allah!
> Ashhadu anna Muhammadan Rasul Allah!
>
> God is great.
> I bear witness that there is no god but Allah.
> I bear witness that Muhammed is his messenger.

These are the first words a Muslim hears upon entering the world — a silent whisper, the azan, breathed into the newborn's ear. A murmur of devotion, ensuring that the first sound to mark their existence is the name of Allah and his messenger, Muhammed. It is an ancient ritual, a thread of faith woven through generations, just as the Prophet once did for the infants of his time, blessing them with words that would shape their souls before they even opened their eyes.

Now, those same words rise again, drifting from the towering minaret into the cool hush of dawn. The village stirs, shadows shifting behind shuttered windows, the world teetering on the edge of sleep and wakefulness. The melody of the call to prayer rolls through the narrow streets, curling around doorways, slipping beneath wooden eaves. A rustling of movement follows — blankets drawn back, feet meeting cold stone, whispered prayers uttered between drowsy breaths.

In the dim glow of lanterns and the silver blush of morning, water splashes softly as the faithful begin their ablutions. Droplets glisten as they run down forearms, slip from fingertips, disappear into the earth. The air hums with quiet reverence. A new day has begun, heralded by the same words that welcomed them into the world.

Then, in perfect unison, they line up behind the imam, bowing and prostrating in absolute silence. Once prayer begins, no one speaks, no one leaves. Men and women worship separately, each lost in devotion.

For the faithful, time itself is measured by these moments of submission. No matter where they are in the world, at the call of the azan, millions of Muslims turn toward the same point: the Kaaba in Mecca. The black cube, which is believed to have been built by Abraham and his son Ishmael, remains the axis of their faith, the focal point of every prayer.

In Dhadar, the villagers followed the Prophet Muhammed's example with unwavering reverence, though few had ever read of his life. Only the learned — like my father, Abba — held such knowledge. For the rest, understanding came through oral tradition. Every Friday, sermons rang out from the minaret's speakers, recounting Muhammed's treatment of the infidels.

And from his words, the laws of their world were born.

All life revolved around Islam, every custom and decision shaped by faith and the Islamic perception of honor, which is totally foreign to the Christian conception of that virtue. In Christianity, honor represents a nobility of spirit and willingness to act bravely in the service of others. In Islam, it is almost the reverse: Honor means upholding the reputation of the community, which Muslims call the *ummah*, above all else. And those who fail in bringing the ummah honor are degraded and, in the worst cases, killed.

Because of this conception of honor, there is little room for individual belief or expression in Muslim society. Instead, every consideration is made for the good of the ummah. In fact, the Koran teaches that Muslims "are the best community that has ever been brought forth for mankind" because, as a collective, "you enjoin what is right and forbid what is wrong and believe in Allah" (sura 3:110). It is everyone's responsibility to protect the integrity of Islam, and a family's honor is measured by how much it succeeds in that mission. Without honor, you have no place in the ummah. Honor stabilizes the community and protects it from harmful un-Islamic influences. And it is for honor's sake that brothers and fathers or even mothers sometimes kill their own daughters or sisters, should they disobey the strict teachings of Muhammed. Indeed, the whole community will work together to either bring the violator back into line or, if she is unwilling to cooperate, destroy her. For an individual to violate the rules — whether by becoming westernized or otherwise breaking the law — is for her to stain the image of the entire community and the honor of Islam. The only redress is revenge. And that is always a community affair.

And so it is that wherever honor is emphasized, so too is death. I once saw a dying man suffer so horribly that the people in the village gathered around him to pray chapters of the Koran to relieve him of his pain. Another time, I showed up at a friend's house where the body of one of her family members was laid out, ritually washed and draped by the women. The continuous presence of death drove home what really mattered in life: to live in fear of Allah and go to Heaven. Islam is very concerned with life after death. From a young age, I was taught that on Judgment Day — what we called *Qiyamat* — there will be a scale on which good deeds are weighed against bad deeds. The Koran tells us that if the good side of the scale is heavy, then you will go to Heaven. And if not, Hell. What's more, Allah's justice is capricious. You can do good deeds all your life, but if you unwittingly did one thing to displease Allah, he may still send you to Hell. And you could have done evil things all your life, but if one thing pleased Allah, then he may send you to Heaven.

The only guaranteed pathway to Paradise was by killing the *Kafir*, infidels. The Koran teaches that the direct path to Paradise is by killing and being killed (Surah 9:111). And those who fight for the cause of Allah will be rewarded with Heaven. Muhammed was said to have declared that "Paradise is under the shades of swords" (Sahih al Bukhari 2818: bk. 56, Hadith 34).

This teaching is deadly serious: If even one believer dies killing a Kafir, his entire family goes to *Jannat* (Heaven). So I was told when I was a child. For that reason, I hated the infidels, the Christians, and the Jews. Everybody I knew hated the Christians and the Jews without anybody having ever met a Christian or a Jew. Hatred for those who reject Islam was a way to please Allah, just like prayer. This, at any rate, was the story we were told as children. This is also why there is no shortage of young men and women to offer themselves for jihad against "the enemies of Islam." I was taught when I was young to memorize the names of those *mujahideen* (martyrs) who died for Allah, who wiped out the infidels, who extinguished countless "impure lives" of the unbelievers. These martyrs were treated like pop stars and their violence toward nonbelievers exalted and glorified.

My story is about how I, the daughter of an entrenched Muslim culture, left Islam and embraced the true Faith, stumbling through Protestant Christianity before finding my home in the Catholic Church. It is intended to be an encouragement to other Muslims seeking Jesus. I have lived through persecutions, physical violence, sexual abuse, death threats, and the loss of my family. I know that, more often than not, there is no one to support you when you leave Islam.

My story is also a warning to the West. Many of the things that Europeans and Americans take for granted are endangered. The gentle way of life in the West is influenced — and even in residual ways still governed — by the way of Christianity. In the Muslim world, things are starker, harsher. And unless the West recognizes what it has in Christianity, it will lose itself to the fastest-growing religion in the world: Islam. This is happening in Europe, and it could very well happen in America. My story is testament both to the strength of Islam and the even greater power of Jesus Christ.

1

Growing Up in Dhadar

I WAS BORN in Dhadar, a small village in the Gujarat District, which is in the extreme northeast of Pakistan. The nearest big city was Lahore, about two hours away. My family was Choudry, which meant we belonged to the landowner caste, and by Pakistani standards, we lived comfortably. Our village was like many villages in rural Pakistan, a jumbled collection of buildings offset from the fields. Everyone worked; the women raised the children and the men provided for the family. Parents showed their love to children by mothers who stayed home with them and cared for them, and children showed their love to their parents by being obedient to their rules. The rhythm of life was measured by religious observance. When we went to the mosque, it was full: We would have to climb over a mountain of shoes, which had to be taken off before entry, to get inside.

My family's house consisted of two buildings joined by a wall at the front. One was my grandfather's house. The other, the bigger one, belonged to my parents. There were few external windows in either building, and all light came from the spacious internal courtyard around which the houses were built. Water was pumped and stored in clay pots daily, which kept it cold. Alongside a pomegranate tree, which the Koran cites as a fruit in Paradise, the courtyard was filled with glorious red hibiscus. And Tota, our talkative and self-important ringneck parrot, frequently flew across the courtyard to greet us as we ate our breakfast. Every morning my mother's routine was the same: She would go outside and light a little fire in the oven — unless it was raining — and begin to make breakfast. All the while, Tota flew around the courtyard and squawked at everything in sight. This was not unusual. Animals and people mixed freely in these spaces.

There were more animals out on our farm. It was a fifteen-minute walk from our house and was called *bahar wala ghar*, which, literally translated, means "the other house." It became difficult to reach when it rained heavily. When this happened, sometimes for days entire areas of our village would be transformed into a trash-filled lake. We would hold each other's hands as we waded through it, since no one in the village could swim. But getting to bahar wala ghar was important. This is where all the animals were kept. We didn't have very many, only a few chickens and three buffalo. And lots of poisonous snakes. I remember going to the farm once and seeing a long white layer of skin in one continuous piece. It filled me with horror that the serpent that had shed this was lurking around somewhere nearby. Another time a snake showed up in our house. I panicked and ran away while others tried to chase it out of the house.

The other houses in Dhadar looked much like ours. They had flat rooftops that, during the warm months, made it easy for us to fall asleep outside while gazing at the carpet of stars in the night sky. Everyone placed beds on the roofs, even though they had no railings. It's a miracle no one ever fell off. And since we were one of the few families in the village who owned a TV, it was convenient for all the neighbors to sit on their roofs and peer into our house to watch a TV drama. But that system was by no means reliable. The power always seemed to fail at the most dramatic moment in the show, leading to a communal sigh of disappointment.

Although we weren't rich, my family enjoyed a special status in the village and the surrounding area because my grandfather — a traditional white-turban-clad man as thin as he was proud — was the local *maulvi*, or scholar of the law. In the morning, he could be heard throughout the village as he called people to morning prayers from the minaret. He performed marriage and funeral ceremonies for the villagers, and our entire family regularly received food donations as a sign of their respect. In Pakistan, religious authorities shape the moral outlook of society, where a person's virtue is defined not by their personal sense of right and wrong but by their obedience to authority and conformity to societal expectations. As an imam, my grandfather naturally held a position of high status and influence.

When the people of Dhadar had a problem, they came to him seeking advice. Wherever Grandfather Aslam would go, people in the shops and on the street would grow silent in his presence, and even we, his family, were filled with great reverence when he entered the house. No one dared to contradict his orders.

Once he told his daughter, Samira, that he wanted her to marry a man whom she had never seen. Samira objected that the man was too old, but Grandfather did not care. In his firm voice he announced loudly to all of us, "This girl should be happy that anyone is willing to accept her." At that moment the matter was final. No one dared to oppose his decision, not even Samira. If Sharia law allows it, who was she to object?

My father, too, had difficulties with my grandfather. He suffered when my grandfather divorced his mother and married a new wife. In Islam a man has only to repeat "I divorce you" three times and the matter is done with! I recall a man in our village who divorced his wife because she liked to tell jokes. But no one dared to question his decision, as he had a theological justification for his actions and had memorized the entire Koran. When my father was a little boy, his stepmother treated him as if he were an orphan, but my grandfather never intervened. A villager later told me that after she married his father, she even refused to buy him shoes. He stood out from his half-siblings growing up because he was the one running around barefoot.

Despite his great strictness, I cared for my grandfather. I was a child and didn't have to make any decisions or have any reason to contradict him. I was pleased when he repeatedly spoke of Allah's blessing on me and told me he hoped that I would become a model student of the Koran. Sometimes I massaged his feet as we all sat around the fire in the cold winters. In these moments he was always a changed man — gentle, loving, and jovial. I never could have imagined that one day he would hold a sickle under my throat and threaten to murder me because I had abandoned his ways.

To Western eyes, my grandfather's sway over my family and our village may seem incredibly jarring, but in fact, it was deeply embedded in Pakistani culture. When I think back on my house, I recall that on our living room wall hung a portrait of General Zia-ul-Haq, who led the way in the Islamization of Pakistan in the late 1970s. His government had instituted many practices, not previously enforced, which transformed the institutions and culture of the country into one of strict religious observance. His was a harsh code. Blasphemy, for instance, which had previously been punishable with life imprisonment, now became a capital offense. The teaching of Islamic studies and Arabic became compulsory. State television was required to broadcast the calls to prayer. More mosques were built. And, crucially, the cruelties already inflicted on women were codified into law.[1] While I was growing up, Zia-ul-Haq died, but the world he built in Pakistan lived on.

---

[1] According to section 8 of the Pakistani penalty code, a woman needs four male witnesses to prove a rape, otherwise she will be charged with *zina* (adultery), the punishment for which is lifelong imprisonment. Most rape cases never make it into the official statistics for this reason, although there are thousands of them. Normally the victims of rape drink poison to take their own lives or end up behind bars for the rest of their lives. Section 8 reads thus: "Proof of zina or zina-bil-jabr: (a) The accused makes a confession of the commission of the offence before a court or competent jurisdiction; or, (b) At least four adult male witnesses, about whom the court is satisfied, having regard

At the same time, Pakistan began exporting its people and customs to Europe. Like many other Pakistanis, my father emigrated to Europe when he was about twenty, in search of a better life. Perhaps he also wanted to escape his stepmother. He soon found that, despite being educated and from an upper caste, he could earn more money doing manual labor in Europe. He ended up in Germany working as a crane operator. After several years, as is the custom, he returned to Pakistan to marry. My mother and father never dated. They got engaged. Everything had been organized between my grandfather and my mother's father.

Despite the fact that the union was arranged, my mother was my father's dream woman. He always called her "Miss," short for Miss Dhadar, because to him she was a beauty queen. "I cannot believe that I am worthy of marrying such a beautiful woman," he always said. Although I've never seen my parents kiss or hug, I always felt their love for each other.

After the wedding, my father stayed on for only a short time before going to Europe. My mother remained behind in my grandfather's house. The taunting of my step-grandmother did not cease when my mother joined the family, and my mother suffered greatly. She often cried in desperation. But she was also very aware of the Pakistani saying: "When you leave the house of your father on your wedding day and go to the house of your husband, you may never go back to your father, no matter how much injustice you experience." So my mother kept all her pain to herself, isolated in a new family with her husband half a world away. My father always took over a year to come home, when he had accumulated enough money to make the costly trip. So many years I waited to see him again. He usually only stayed for a few weeks upon his return. Then he went back to his new work in Austria.

---

to the requirement that the witness is a truthful person and abstains from major sins, give evidence as eyewitnesses of the act of penetration necessary to the offence."

About every two years my mom would become pregnant and have a child. In all, there were four of us: I was the oldest, then my two brothers, then my little sister. Taking care of four children was a big challenge for my mother — duties that came in addition to helping with the family farm. The electricity went out every two hours. Water had to be pumped by hand each day and heated on a *chula*, a clay oven. Wood had to be collected in the forest to make fires for the chula. There were no diapers or dishwashers. As soon as I could walk, I had to look after my younger siblings and help with the household chores. I always carried my younger brothers around in my arms. If I wanted to play with my friends, I took my brothers along. I was proud to have two brothers — my mother always reminded me that brothers protect sisters when they grow up. But as my brothers grew older, I noticed that they didn't have to do any chores. When I asked my mother, she simply replied, "They are men, you are a woman. That's just the way it is."

My mother lost her own mother when she was born, and she had no memory of her — not even a photo, since the imam thought picture-taking was sinful — and she grew up surrounded by violence. Her father was a strict man. Her older sister, who was tasked with raising her three siblings, was not able to give the love of a mother. When I was born, my mother told me that no one was very happy, because I was a girl. That's how life was: Young men were prized more than women. I still remember clearly how badly one of my friends was beaten when she failed to make a fried egg properly. Her mother dressed her down right in front me, hitting her repeatedly. In some extreme cases, girls are discarded simply for not being boys.

There was a strict order of things in Dhadar. All of life was lived publicly. No one locked their doors. No one made appointments, because the women were always at home to receive you. Strangers on a journey and passing through town frequently stayed in our house, knowing we were the family of the imam. The village saw itself as one extended family. Relatives and visitors who came for dinner were always given the opportunity to stay, sometimes even for months if they wanted. And from a very early age, my mother made clear to me my role in that family's order: that of a housewife, there to serve the men in the family. Had I been born a hundred years earlier, my early childhood wouldn't have been much different. There were hardly any cars; the roads were made of dust and dirt, traversed by horse carts and bicycles. We woke every morning at sunrise to the call of prayer and went to sleep as the fire died each evening. The line of my life had been drawn out clear and straight — just as easily as it had been for my mother and for her mother before her.

And yet I had a defiant streak in me. I was born with an inherent sense of justice and the will to stand up for myself — even if it meant getting hurt. And for a woman in Pakistan, it could mean much worse. Our neighbor, Faiza, endured a great deal of suffering. Despite everything, she was always kind to me. At the time, I was just eight years old. Sometimes, when I visited her, she offered me food. Other times she would just weep: I frequently heard her scream in terror and pain from the violent beatings received from her husband, Sajeed. One day I witnessed Sajeed kicking her so brutally that I thought he would break her bones. No one dared to intervene. Feeling incredibly sorry, I ran over to her house, but I was unable to help. Everyone knew about Faiza's plight, but no one did anything about it.

There was, however, one place where I was always obedient and excelled: the classroom. Only a few children in our village went to school, as there was no obligation to attend and many families in my village simply couldn't afford it. Every morning, with a couple of other girls from my class, I walked four kilometers to the neighboring village of Dhunni, which had the only decent school in the area. It was a primary school at which English, Urdu, mathematics, gymnastics, and religion were taught. I enjoyed school, but my greatest desire was to search for Allah and to go to Paradise. I was especially good at learning the Koran. In fact, I must have been only ten years old when I first read the entire Koran in Arabic. My best friend, Deira, was not as gifted, so she turned to Allah for help. Before exams, she would drink out of her special cup, on the outside of which were written verses from the Koran while the inside was gold-plated. Naturally, she believed that when she prayed to Allah and sought out his blessing, he would look fondly on her and prevent her from failing.

Deira lived three houses down from my family, and I would stop by her house daily and we would walk to school together. I may have been the better student, but I adored the way she carried herself because, unlike me, she was reserved and shy. And in Islam timid women are considered virtuous. She had a charming personality and was a good companion for the long, daily walk to school. It was a good day if we managed to get to school without taking any breaks, as we would often stop along the way to buy DalSevian, a Pakistani snack food made from chickpea flour.

In the hot summer, temperatures can exceed 125 degrees Fahrenheit. I would take frequent rest breaks, but even then, I would cry from exhaustion. Fasting from water and food for fifteen to eighteen hours a day and, depending on your location, for an entire month, is a test of faith and fortitude for every Muslim. I was far from alone in my discomfort. However, the situation became even more unbearable for many people when Ramadan, the annual thirty-day period when every Muslim is supposed to fast from dawn to dusk, fell in summertime. During that month, eating and drinking — including water — is strictly prohibited. And in Dhadar everyone took Ramadan seriously, because the practice is obligatory for all Muslims except those who are sick or traveling. No water or food passed our lips from dawn to dusk.

Ramadan is the holiest month of Islam. It is believed that during that time the Koran was sent down from Heaven, and it marks the prophethood of Muhammed. Muhammed was born around 570 in Mecca. His father Abdullah died before his birth, and his mother Amina died when he was six. Muhammed was raised by his uncle Abu Talib and became a merchant, in which capacity he came into contact with Jews and Christian sects. He later married his first wife Kahdija, who was also the businesswoman that he worked for. Muhammed used to spend much time in solitude in the Cave of Hira. According to Islamic tradition, the first verses of the Koran were revealed to him there through the angel Gabriel. Muhammed was very confused afterward, and even suicidal, because he thought that he had been attacked by demons. But his wife Kahdija convinced him that he was a prophet, and she became his first follower.

At the end of Ramadan is Eid al-Fitr, one of the most important dates on the Muslim calendar, when the faithful sacrifice a lamb, goat, or cow to Allah. The sacrifice commemorates that of the prophet Ibrahim (Abraham), who was prepared to sacrifice his son Ismail (Ishmael) after seeing in a dream that Allah wanted him to do so. The dream, however, was a test from Allah, and he sent down a ram from Heaven to be sacrificed in Ismail's place. This story, even with its curious editing and material change of detail and meaning, is of course familiar to Christians and Jews from the Old Testament. For Muslims, it means that by sacrificing an animal each year at the end of Ramadan, every Muslim reconfirms that he is willing to sacrifice whatever Allah asks for and that he is willing to submit to Allah completely.

Needless to say, Eid was always a huge feast in Dhadar, and the slaughtered animals were shared with the whole community.

During the summer holidays our little village practically doubled in size, since the families who had moved abroad came back to visit. Several children from Dhadar had moved to England with their families over the years and, when they returned, we would rush to gather around them and listen to their stories of this different world. They were always beautifully dressed, and some of them even wore Western clothes, such as jeans. Meanwhile, I, who had never left Pakistan, only ever wore a *salwar kameez*, a long blouse reaching below the knee over loose pants.

The girls had lots to tell us, and we were an eager audience, hungry to hear about the music, the clothes, school — everything about their life in England. It was as if these girls were pop stars. They seemed so foreign, simply because they were dressed so differently and had been to such faraway places. I wanted nothing more than to be like them.

Europe seemed like a paradise to me. I thought it was a place where everybody had lots of money, drove fancy cars, and wore expensive clothes. My father reinforced this impression with photos he would send us of the pretty, clean landscape dotted with huge houses. When he visited, he would also bring us sweets that I had never eaten before.

When I was about eight years old, my father moved from Germany to Austria, where he worked for a construction company. Once, he sent a picture of himself operating a crane. We were in awe. The whole family got together in the house and admired this amazing contraption, and everybody fought for a chance to hold the photo. My grandfather was so proud of his son for being able to operate this strange machine, and my mother believed that her husband's ability to control such a beast meant he really must have made it in Europe. She ran from house to house showing the picture to all the neighbors. Nobody was able to explain exactly what my father was doing with the crane, but nobody cared either.

When my father returned for the summer holidays that year, he said that he would soon take us back to Austria with him. I was ten years old when his promise finally came true, and my life changed completely.

One day I arrived home from school to find a motorbike parked in the courtyard. Although we often had visitors, only very rarely did anybody come with a motorbike. I went to see who it was and found the postman handing my grandfather an important-looking package. My grandfather took the letter and spent what felt to me like hours opening it, reading it, and generally investigating its contents. Finally, he pulled out visas for my mother, my siblings, and me. I had never been so excited in my life — it was finally happening! We were going to Austria, and we would finally all be together! Even my grandfather, who rarely showed his feelings, was visibly happy, so we knew this was something really special.

It was only a few weeks later, in September 1992, when we started out on our journey. With visas and passports in hand, we were to fly from Lahore to Karachi, then on to Dubai, and from there to Vienna. When my father came back to collect us, it took only a few hours to pack up the most important items. The night before we drove to Lahore, I couldn't sleep because of all the excitement. It was no longer a fantasy: This was my new life. Yet I didn't know what I would find. I wondered how the people talked there and how I would understand them. I had learned a few English phrases at school, but I didn't speak a single word of German. How would I make friends? What would our house look like? What would we eat? I had heard about strange fruits in Austria with names like "cherry" and "strawberry," but I didn't have the faintest idea what they looked or tasted like. I knew only watermelons and mangoes, which grew in every Pakistani garden.

I was also worried about what clothes I would wear. Up to this point I had almost exclusively worn a salwar kameez, which every Pakistani woman wears (I had lots of these), and I was used to running around the village barefoot. But I knew I would need shoes, jeans, and T-shirts to fit in with the Western girls. That much I had learned from the girls in our village who visited from England. It was all so exciting, but I also had no idea of the perils my new life would carry with it.

2

MOVING TO THE WEST

IT WAS LATE afternoon when we finally arrived in Sarleinsbach, a little village tucked away in the hills of Upper Austria. The village was not far from Salzburg, where Wolfgang Amadeus Mozart was born, though of course most Americans probably know Salzburg as the home of the von Trapp family, made so famous by *The Sound of Music*. When my family moved to Sarleinsbach, it was home to about 2,300 people. The village was more than 1,200 years old, and the old market square, with its stone building and angular streets leading into it, was still its center. At the very middle of Sarleinsbach stood a Catholic church, St. Peter's, which even then was the heart of the village.

When we arrived, we drove through the village, turned left off the main street, and then wound slowly up a country lane. "Our new home is up there," my father said, pointing. I couldn't believe my eyes. For the first time, I saw forests that had trees with sharp needles. On top of a hill stood the most beautiful house I had ever seen: a large farmhouse of white stone with a black shingle roof. The farm wasn't new, but its age made it seem even more impressive. In front of the house, there was a large garden with a huge apple tree. The air was clear and free: At many hours I could hear, instead of the voice of my grandfather singing the call of prayer through the minaret speakers, the peaceful melodies of church bells over long distances. Down in the valley, a stream cut through the landscape. Everything about the place was wonderful.

My father and his friend were still unloading the bags from the car when my brothers and I ran into the house. There were countless rooms, including a bathroom with a toilet that looked like nothing we had at home. And there was a kitchen with a wood-burning stove. What a sensation! What luxury! So, I thought to myself, this is where I'm going to live. I was happier than I'd ever been.

My mother, on the other hand, was far more skeptical. As my siblings and I ran around exploring, she approached the house slowly and looked around with fear. When she entered the kitchen, she completely lost her composure. My father had already been living in the house for some months, but he had never really bothered with cooking since he had never learned how. The place was not well-provisioned: There were only a few glasses and plates and hardly any saucepans to cook for a family. My mother burst into tears, turned on her heel, and stormed out.

In our house in Pakistan, there had been no modern kitchen equipment, but everything was organized in a very functional way. My mother was master of the kitchen; she always had everything under control. It was my father's job to provide for her so that she could look after the household. Here there was nothing for her: no cutlery, no saucepans, no familiar equipment.

"How am I going to cook here?" she sobbed.

At just that moment, a stocky woman much older than my mother came up the path. Her short hair was streaked white, and she seemed powerful, yet friendly. She didn't look like any woman I'd ever seen before. It wasn't just the short hair. She wore trousers.

"I'm Frieda," she said.

When Frieda saw my mother sobbing, she asked my father what was wrong. He told her about the lack of saucepans, and Frieda turned around without a word. She went back to her house and returned moments later with a few old cooking pots, which she gave my mother as a present. But before she used the pots, my mother washed them three times and spoke *bismillah*, an Islamic prayer, over them. She had to do this because Frieda wasn't a Muslim and could have cooked pork in them, which is *haram*, impure, in Islam.

We arrived in Sarleinsbach about a week before school started, and during this period I explored the area. Directly across from us lived married farmers, Rosi and Sepp. They were kind people and, particularly during the first few weeks, paid a lot of attention to their new neighbors. They had a daughter who was unmarried but had a child. I couldn't wrap my head around this.

"But she's a nice woman," I said to my mother. "Why does she shame her family like that, having a child even though she's not married?"

In Pakistan, Rosi's daughter would have been strangled or soaked in gasoline and set alight for destroying her family's honor. I was sure that she had done wrong and was for that reason always especially careful when our paths crossed. As I have said, in Pakistan, honor is the most important family value, and it depends primarily on the behavior of women and how closely they follow Islamic tradition. I had been taught that if I disappointed my parents, I would bring shame to my entire family, even though I was in Austria and they were in Pakistan. It did not matter that Rosi's daughter was a nice woman and that nobody ostracized her or called her shameful names; I still chose to avoid her. Unconditional love is nonexistent in Islam: Those who disobey its rules must be punished. That parents could love a daughter even though she had sinned was a new, frightening idea for me.

I felt much safer with Frieda. She was retired and lived with her son, Max, and his wife, Maria, in a farmhouse directly below our hill. Max had a large workshop where he made horse carriages. Maria worked as well, which seemed very unusual to me. Frieda was one of the most important people to me at that time. I was at her house almost every day, and I called her "Mama" because I didn't know what else to call her. In Pakistan a younger person is not allowed to address an older person by name. But adapting those rules to Austrian life proved challenging.

Should I refer to Frieda as "Mrs."? That seemed too impersonal. Auntie? She was too old for that, and, besides, I already had far too many aunts. So Mama became my first friend in Austria.

Frieda showed my mother and me around the village, introduced us to other people, and even went shopping with us. She was there for us whenever we needed anything. She taught me my first few words of German. Thanks to Frieda, I was at least able to say "hello" and "goodbye" on my first day of primary school.

On that day, I entered the classroom shortly before 8:00 a.m., wearing my yellow salwar kameez, which I had worn on the trip to Austria. All the other children were already there. It was a large classroom in an old schoolhouse, built in 1966, with tables, chairs, and a blackboard. I looked around. Not one of the other children wore anything that remotely resembled a salwar kameez.

The teacher welcomed me and smiled in a friendly way. Naturally, I had no idea what he was saying. He motioned me to come to him. Then he took my hand and led me around the room. I felt strange, like an elephant at the zoo. All the other children stared at me with huge eyes, which wasn't really surprising: Just as I had never seen a full classroom with proper tables and chairs, they had never seen a Pakistani girl with brown skin, dark hair, and a flowing, yellow salwar kameez.

I squeezed my teacher's hand as he took me through the room and showed me to my seat. And there was the next surprise: Sitting next to me was a boy. In Pakistan this would have been unimaginable. Not only that boys and girls were taught in the same classes together but that they even sat beside each other on their benches.

The first few days at school were quite difficult for me as I didn't understand a single word of what was being said. But thanks to my teacher and, above all, Frieda, I made rapid progress. After only a few weeks, I found that I was better at arithmetic than the Austrian children and, in gym class, I could climb the poles faster. I'd spent entire afternoons climbing the trees in our fields back in Dhadar; my poor Austrian classmates had not been so lucky.

The girls were fascinated by my hair, which was a lot thicker and more voluminous than theirs. They couldn't believe it was real. When I let them run their hands over it, they stared and giggled, which I always found nice. It was less nice when they asked me why I and my family dressed so strangely. I told them my outfit was called a salwar kameez and that I didn't have anything else to wear, prompting the girls to look at me pityingly.

When I told my mother about this, she agreed to buy me Western clothing. The same day, we drove with my father to the nearby city of Linz and went into a popular clothing store. I had never been in a shop like this before. There were fantastic things everywhere: jeans, T-shirts, jumpers, jackets, made of all sorts of different materials in all sorts of different colors. Loud pop music played over speakers, and the sales staff, wearing stylish outfits themselves, helped me figure out my size and try on all sorts of cool clothes. That day I got my first pair of jeans and a sweatshirt. Somehow, I'd made it: Now I looked like the girls from England who came back to visit Pakistan.

Initially, I had hardly any contact with the Austrian children, as my family kept very much to ourselves. I woke up early with my parents, though it felt unusual not to hear the call to prayer echoing from the minaret. When my father drove off to work, I got ready to go to school. After the last class, I walked home straight away, which meant thirty minutes of walking each day and sometimes a full hour since my mother couldn't drive. After eating, I spent hours playing with my brothers in the fields, as lower grades in Austria rarely lasted more than three to four hours. We played tag and soccer, chased the neighbor's goat, and explored our new home. It only took one shock for me to learn not to touch the electric fence surrounding our neighbor's field.

After one year, I started my secondary education in public school, another culture shock. The school year began, as it always did, with Mass.

This was the first time I entered a Catholic church. How different it was to me! The inside of the church was ornate, decorated with statues of Christ and His mother and the saints placed there over the centuries. And how strange the Mass seemed! In Islam, we prostrate ourselves five times a day before God. It is always the same ritual: You turn your body toward Mecca, the holy city of Islam, and, with your forehead touching the ground, recite your prayers. At my first Mass, I didn't understand what the priest was doing, but even then, I knew he was speaking in reverent tones. I was surprised that even Christians kneel when they pray.

Every day in the classroom, the children started off by praying the Our Father while looking at the crucifix. I was fascinated by that. I think I must have — almost without knowing it — connected the image of suffering I saw on the cross to that of Faiza back in Dhadar. There, people had gathered around her and other women who had been beaten and accused of disobeying the laws of Muhammed. Here, people prayed to someone beaten and humiliated, and they called him their God. The contrast was stark.

Meanwhile, my studies progressed rapidly, and I no longer had any problems with the language. In fact, I could read and write as well as my classmates and was at the top of the class in German. I spoke nearly as strong a dialect as they did. If someone were to listen to me with their eyes closed, they could have taken me for a local wearing a *dirndl*, the traditional Austrian clothing.

My parents were very proud of how well I did in school and were pleased that I had decided I wanted to be a doctor. For Pakistani girls of my caste, there are three acceptable professions: doctor, lawyer, or teacher. However, the point was not to pursue any of these careers for their own sake, but to have those degrees to make you more impressive to your husband's family. This was my path as well: I would get a degree in medicine, and then I would return to Pakistan to be a good wife.

At the time I had two very good friends, Elisabeth and Katharina. Both lived close to my family's house. We were in the same class and although both were a year younger than I, we got on really well together. Like me, Katharina loved pop music. Unlike me, she was allowed to put up posters of her favorite bands all over her wall. My mother always said that because I was a girl I was not allowed to admire a boy — even on a poster — or I would go to Hell.

Katharina's parents had an enormous house, and we went there almost every day after school. Elisabeth and Katharina seldom came to my house because my mother didn't like having Austrian visitors. At home, I spent most of my time looking after my younger brothers and sister. My mother wasn't particularly keen on us mixing with Austrians. Even after a year, she refused to learn "these people's" language. Taking care of us four children took up most of her time. One of my brothers, my father, or I had to go with her to help her do the grocery shopping. When Austrians were friendly to her, she was friendly in return, but when out of earshot she would bluntly state that "these people" were unclean because they ate pork and drank alcohol. She was also very concerned with family honor and therefore refrained from doing anything that would have involved coming into contact with male strangers. There were two other Pakistanis in Sarleinsbach, friends of my father. My mother might have been afraid they would criticize her for leaving the house without my father's permission. In any case, my mother found Austrian society rather decadent.

Once we were in Austria, my mother openly complained to my father if something didn't suit her. They still had a very strong relationship, but now there was no mother-in-law to punish her for her misbehavior. And whereas my mother had occasionally worn the burka in Pakistan, she never wore one in Austria. Nevertheless, she maintained a chaste and traditional appearance and behaved like other good Muslim women. She did not look at men and lowered her eyes whenever she interacted with them. My mother restricted herself to her role as housewife, focusing on cooking and cleaning. In the small village where she came from, women learned the Koran and submission but not how to make their own decisions, so it was very difficult for my mother to accept our adaptation to Western culture. In her mind, it was her responsibility to behave in the Islamic way and guard her family's reputation.

Her demeanor changed only when we had visitors, Pakistani visitors. One of the two other Pakistanis in town was Ahmed, the man who had collected us from the airport and worked at the same construction company as my father. Ahmed was a Muslim scholar. He had neither a wife nor a family yet, which didn't appear to upset him. He had us instead. Ahmed also used to perform the *qurbani* at our house, when after Eid al-Adha, at the end of Ramadan, we always sacrificed a lamb. It was quite a traumatic event. We used to play with the animal beforehand. Then we would watch Ahmed kill it with the *halal* method. First, prayers were said, then the throat of the animal was pierced. While the poor animal shook, its blood was drained before its head was chopped off. We always watched the whole ordeal.

When we first arrived in Austria, I wrote to my cousins and my old schoolmates almost every week. We missed having our extended family around, and I used to cry because I missed my grandparents so much. Every time we received a letter from Pakistan, it was a celebration. My father would read it aloud in Urdu as we sat around him, listening intently. But over time the letters I wrote back became fewer and fewer. I was becoming increasingly independent and preferred to spend my time with Elisabeth and Katharina. We met after school to chat and listen to music. I started to speak less and less Urdu. I spoke to my father and my siblings mostly in German. Even when my mother, who still didn't speak any German, wanted something from me, I made no effort to talk to her in Urdu. Within two or three years I had become a true Austrian, even if I didn't yet have Austrian citizenship.

My parents rarely complained about how I'd adapted to our new life. Although they lived a traditional Pakistani life, there were only a few things that I was not allowed to do. It was obvious that they trusted me. Why should they not have? I fasted during Ramadan, prayed the *namaz* (the daily prayers, also known as *salah*), and read the Koran. And each time I read it, my heart became more filled with hatred for the infidels, which caused a conflict in me: I was supposed to hate my friends and neighbors who loved me so much. I helped my mother around the house whenever she asked me to. As before, I went shopping with her, washed the dishes, and helped her with the laundry. I did what was expected of me. The only prohibition that disturbed me a little was that I was never allowed to stay overnight with Elisabeth or Katharina, but even that I could live with.

Otherwise, I gave my parents no cause for concern because for me, the onset of puberty wasn't a particularly difficult time. I was born into the family of a mullah, so belief in Allah constituted the center of my life. I was a good Muslim: I did not think of myself as an individual; I considered myself a member of the ummah. And even though my surroundings in Austria were so different from those in Pakistan, my identity was essentially the same. Islam determined what I could eat and drink, what I could wear, who were my friends and enemies, and who I would eventually marry. My parents trusted that I would continue to be a good Pakistani girl and were convinced I would never question the religion of Allah.

For me — and for all other Muslims — the words of Prophet Muhammed were always present. He may have died fifteen hundred years before me, but I wanted to be like him. We were told that Muhammed was the greatest man who ever lived on earth and a role model for all mankind. The Koran says that Muhammed was the most exemplary follower of Allah: "Indeed, in the messenger of Allah you have an excellent example" (Koran 33:21). All good Muslims felt this way, and the most wonderful thing in life was to be as holy as the Prophet and then eventually to go to Heaven, a land of milk and honey, where there is no suffering, no poverty: a paradise. When I was barely a teenager in Sarleinsbach, I was thinking along these lines. How would I achieve

Paradise — did I have the courage to be a martyr for Allah? I wasn't so sure. I didn't think I was ready to give my life for anyone.

Instead, I tried to impress Allah with my piety and capacity for sacrifice. One day when I was in gym class, I nearly fainted for lack of water. Immediately a classmate offered me her water bottle. But I refused: I wasn't about to share a drink with a Christian. And I was convinced that the angel of Allah had seen that sacrifice and that I would one day be rewarded in Paradise for it. Another time, in history class, the subject of Islam came up. The teacher, a middle-aged woman, constantly spoke of "Muhammed" and "the Muhammadens." This made me furious. I stood up and called out, "We are not Muhammadens, we are Muslims. And you can't just call the Prophet by his name, you have to say 'Muhammed, peace be upon him.'" The teacher was surprised by my angry outburst. But she responded with kindness which, in turn, surprised me.

I recount these stories because for me and for my family, the idea of Austria as a land of infidels was a visceral reality. My father was always repeating the same refrain: "Look at the Christians: their churches are empty, and their brothels are full. They dump their parents in old-age homes, they don't want responsibility." When he said this, I felt even prouder to be Muslim — even though Sarleinsbach was welcoming and few people there fit that description of infidel. It surprised me that there was no trace of racism or anti-Muslim sentiment in Sarleinsbach. On the contrary, I was the intolerant one.

Still, the country's atmosphere was intoxicating. I loved living in Sarleinsbach — planting potatoes with Frieda, marveling at the beauty of the mountains, and watching the apple trees bloom and picking their fruits with my brothers while the leaves changed color. My life in Austria was idyllic, like a scene from *The Sound of Music*. And indeed, like Maria in that film, I loved to sing, no matter the song, and to hike through the breathtaking passes of the Alps. I remember on one occasion climbing up a mountain in Hinterstoder, also called the "pearl of the Alps." I felt like I was drowning in beauty. The trail, like many in the Alps, had a crucifix at its summit, whose significance I would only come to appreciate when I was much older. But even then, I could not help but notice that the cross was present everywhere: in the church, the classrooms, in Frieda's house, at the beautiful cemetery that I used to pass through every day. Now that I have suffered some, it reminds me ever more clearly of God's ultimate sacrifice for our sins.

Sweet Jesus on the Cross,
Blessed be the day my eyes first beheld you,
Man of sorrows, ever near, ever true.
Whether I wandered 'cross hills, where wildflowers bloom,
Or by the stream in the valley's silent gloom,
You were there, unbidden, yet never far.

Why, O Light Divine, when you came to me,
Did you unveil a face so bruised, so broken?
Are you not the image of your Father's beauty?

Why were you helpless, nailed upon a piece of wood?
Is pain the very name of your revelation?
Like the 99 names of Allah,
Is this one of yours?

When I sought the truth, was I seeking you, O Jesus?
And knowing the depths of my longing,
Did you run toward me to win my heart?

Did you call to me, Beloved, as I passed,
Whispering softly though I could not hear:
"Behold, daughter, my Holy Face —
Gaze upon me and see the Truth.
One day, this crown of thorns shall save you.
You shall bear the cross that I am nailed to;

The many beatings that I endure,
You will suffer in your body.

I was spat upon, and so shall you be.
Betrayed, abandoned, as I once was too.
The friends I loved have fled from me,
And so, daughter, they shall forsake you.
The very ones I cherished, gave me scorn —
I am condemned to die for truth, for love,
Be not surprised when it comes to you

Out of millions have I called you —
to follow me where I am most alone. To Golgotha.

I have many admirers,
But I chose you to be my friend,
A friend of my Passion."

3

A Taste of Freedom

One day in the spring of 1996 my father came home and announced that he had a new job and that we would be moving to Linz in a few weeks. I didn't know how to react. On the one hand, I was thirteen and excited about living in a city, although I had little idea of what that would mean other than that I would be able to go to a proper high school. On the other hand, I really liked living in Sarleinsbach. I had my friends, our neighbor Frieda was there, and I knew the village and enjoyed my well-regulated life. I was comfortable.

My mother had no reservations. She had grown increasingly lonely in Sarleinsbach, largely because she didn't speak the language and struggled to communicate with the Austrians. It was difficult for her because in the village where she grew up, there were only Muslims, and in Pakistan, Muslims generally don't befriend non-Muslims. She hoped that in Linz all of this would change.

We moved only a few weeks later. My father had rented an apartment in Wiener Strasse on the seventh floor of a huge building. It was a good neighborhood on a busy street. Although the city was a relatively small provincial one, to me it seemed large, bustling, and cosmopolitan. Linz, Austria's third-largest city and the capital of Upper Austria, sits on the banks of the Danube River and was founded by the Romans. It is located midway between Salzburg and Vienna. Much of the architecture is baroque and the Old Town is picturesque — filled with small shops in centuries-old buildings and lined with cobblestone streets. Unlike

Sarleinsbach, Linz seemed like home for the whole world. There were people there from all over the globe, even Africa.

Most of the immigrants had come in the 1960s as *Gastarbeiter* (guest workers) to help address a labor shortage, just as they had in other European countries such as Germany, Sweden, and France. The various European governments at the time assumed that they would leave when their work was done. They were wrong. Most stayed, just like my father. And then they brought their families over to join them and take advantage of the quality of life, the order and safety, and better schooling. And yet, though they enjoyed these benefits, most of the migrants — predominantly Muslim — rejected the Christian culture that had produced this stability. Unlike immigrants from within Europe, Muslims from Turkey, Pakistan, and North African countries had no desire to assimilate. They took advantage of Europe's riches while despising its culture.

My family was a typical example of this tendency. Our apartment in Linz was as Pakistani as we could make it. We had three rooms — a living room, where my brothers also slept, a bedroom for my parents, and another for my sister and me. We had no pictures, only stitched Arabic phrases hung on the walls: the name of Allah on one side and the name of Muhammed on the other. Right beneath these my father placed his carefully selected editions of the Hadith of Sahih Al Buchari. The Hadith describe what most Muslims, and the mainstream school of Islamic thought, believe to be the words and deeds of the Prophet Muhammed.[2]

---

[2] Islam cannot be practiced without the Hadith. Both the Sunni and Shia establishments agree that a Muslim needs to believe in the Koran and Sunna (the body of customs based on the Hadith). In this book, all quotations from the Hadith will be from sources that the mainstream Islamic schools recognize as "authentic." The Sunni denomination comprises approximately 90 percent of Muslims. Because my family too was Sunni, all interpretations of Islam in this book are from the mainstream Sunni understanding. This is important because sometimes people in the West are fooled by some very moderate versions of Islam, but they represent a small minority. To believe them and

My school was different too: more Muslim. Still, I was the only Pakistani. The others came from Bosnia, Turkey, and Iran. And here, no one prayed to the man on the cross. Rather, we had our own separate Islamic education funded by the state. We Muslims were proud of our faith and culture, and no one ever dared to challenge us. In fact, the Austrian kids seemed to lack any confidence about their own culture. And if they had shown any, we had a powerful weapon at our disposal: the accusation of racism. They couldn't speak about us, let alone criticize us. In keeping with the school's embrace of multiculturalism, discussions about Islam and the Prophet Muhammed were restricted to Muslims only. Of course, this was not an official policy. But it didn't need to be; everyone knew it and behaved accordingly.

Many of the Austrians in Linz came from secularized homes and weren't sure how to respond to us. Sometimes when blonde Austrian children entered the room, we Muslims, emboldened by our numbers, shouted at them: "Immigrants out!" One of the Muslim students, Ali, was particularly flagrant. Before a test he would raise his hand and tell the teacher that Islam demanded he pray before he proceeded — a flat lie. The teacher, Mrs. Krenn, who wanted to be extra tolerant, would grant his request. The others just rolled their eyes, but Ali impressed me: He demonstrated that Mrs. Krenn was a weak Christian. And even though the victory was small, it confirmed our belief that Islam would triumph over Christianity and the West.

In our Islamic religion class, the Muslim teacher Mrs. Amina wore a headscarf, which pleased me enormously. We were told that if we the Muslim children ever faced any issues, we could go to Mrs. Amina since she best understood the cultural differences. She always presented a liberal face to the secular and Christian Austrian community. However, within the Muslim community she taught a social order according to

---

their version of Islam is like believing that Jehovah's Witnesses speak for Christianity.

Sharia law—especially when it came to the role of women. She was not a liberal Muslim.

My brothers went to the same secondary school as I did, but unlike me they spent most of their afternoons on the soccer field, just like in Sarleinsbach. I, on the other hand, wasn't allowed to do things with my Christian classmates. Islam forbids true friendship with Christians. The Koran teaches: "O you who believe. Do not take friends from the Christians and Jews. They are friends to each other. And if anyone among you befriends them, then surely he is one of them!" A few times I fought for one of my Austrian girlfriends to come to our house. My mother was unfailingly polite and friendly to them and served them all sorts of foods. But as soon as they left, she opened the windows — "because they stink" — and purified the dishes they had eaten off of.

Those first few months in Linz were a test of centuries of Islamic teaching and practice. It had been ingrained in me that a young Muslim girl's place was at home helping her mother. Being independent and going your own individual way, like people do in the West, was an idea utterly foreign to me. Even if I had wanted to act differently, the ummah would have prevented me. The wider Muslim community regards itself as the guardian of how other members of the community behave — always watching to see if they adopt Western values, such as secularism, which doesn't exist in the Muslim world. Most Muslims believe that this arrangement is for the best: They see that Christians don't have strong community bonds as they do. Muslims have security and comfort, even if it means having no individual freedom. They prefer that to the isolated existence of contemporary secular culture. And in the beginning, these too were the rules of my life: I would go home after school, help my mother, and look after my little sister, who was still at primary school and was a lively, well-behaved child who laughed a lot and idolized me.

Abba still worked as a crane operator with a construction company and took a second job as a taxi driver. I often felt sorry for him that despite his good education he had to do two jobs. He worked a lot and was seldom at home. He felt responsible for earning money not just to provide for the family here, but also for our relatives in Pakistan. He also dreamed of returning to Pakistan and building a big house for us there.

It was my mother who blossomed most obviously in our new environment. Now that we lived in the same city as her Pakistani women friends, she was much happier than she had been for years. She had learned a little German and would even dare to venture out to the little market on her own if she ran out of sugar or flour. We had guests regularly, whom my mother served lovingly with traditional Pakistani dishes. She was a good cook. When guests arrived at our house, the whole apartment was filled with the scent of curry and Bollywood music. It was easy to see how happy she was with Linz and her new Islamic community — and I was pleased for her.

Even though Linz is the capital of Upper Austria, it was only a short while before we knew every Pakistani family in the city. Every time my father came home from the mosque, he had made new friends.[3] And now that my mother had people like her in the same city, she was able to isolate herself completely from Christians and continued to live as if she were still in Pakistan. This is how most Muslims in Linz lived. We built a parallel Muslim society within the city. And, as the number of immigrants grew, so did the strength and resilience of this parallel

---

[3] In this mosque, money was collected for Hamas, the terror organization that on October 7, 2023, murdered thousands of Jews, including babies, and kidnapped hundreds of innocent Jewish men, women, and children. Like most Muslims, I saw Hamas simply as an extension of the community. I once heard a Muslim from our community say, "Hitler has only left a handful of Jews behind, and they are polluting the world." Muslims believe that the day of judgment will only come when Muslims fight the Jews and eliminate them. Indeed, the Prophet Muhammed said: "The hour of judgment shall not come unless the Muslims fight the Jews and kill them, so that the Jews hide behind trees and stones, and each tree and stone will say; 'Oh Muslim, oh slave of Allah, there is a Jew behind me, come and kill him'" (Sahih Muslim 2922).

society. Even though they were living in a country with law and justice, no one really cared for it. They felt that those were Christian, not Muslim, rules and as such irrelevant. The ummah had law and justice that was — and is — regularly applied to individuals who did not conform.

This way of life has its benefits, and when you are in good standing in the Muslim community, it is even pleasant. We got together for dinner parties several times a month with our new family friends. During Ramadan we took turns inviting each other for the *iftar*, the breaking of the fast. Hospitality is a big part of Islam and is rooted in the sayings of Muhammed, who proclaimed: "Whoever believes in Allah and the Last day, entertains his guest." And it also goes back to the story of Abraham and Sarah, who took in strangers and hosted them. This stood in contrast to the Christians, who only offered hospitality conditionally. When I was a child, a Muslim man I knew used to say: "When you go to the Christians' homes, take a piece of toast with you! They won't offer you anything." Hospitality is one of the most beautiful aspects of Islam, and I have never seen anything like it anywhere else in the world.

Out of all our new friends, I was especially pleased when Farah and her family came by. The father was a store manager at McDonald's, and the mother, like most Pakistani women, was a housewife. They lived only a few tram stops away from us. Farah was my age and loved the Backstreet Boys as much as I did. She also had posters all over her walls. I was still not allowed to hang pictures of strange men — my mother called them idols. When Farah visited, we could discuss the latest gossip we had read in *Bravo*, a teen magazine she would sneak in. I was allowed to go to her house and even spend the night once. We spent hours watching Bollywood movies. And, though her family seemed more liberal than mine, my parents were really impressed with Farah because she wore the salwar kameez, even in Linz. They thought she was the epitome of a good Pakistani girl. But Farah was not as chaste as she seemed. In *Bravo*, there were always two pages with a picture of a naked girl and a naked boy and a column about sex and contraception. She would glue the pages together in case her parents ever found it — but only after reading them.

I was also friends with another Pakistani girl named Razia. My parents approved of her because, while she had been raised in Austria, she had received a good education, defended Islam, and acted very chaste and uninterested in boys. At least that's what they thought. In reality, Razia had a Muslim boyfriend whom she met for trysts in a hotel. He was Pakistani, and they were eventually married. Everyone in the community believed she was a virgin on her wedding night. This was standard — modest, well-behaved Pakistani girls who secretly had boyfriends — though not without danger. Young Muslim women are not supposed to date, a practice that is thought to open too many possibilities of threats to the community. Besides, Sharia law doesn't allow a Muslim woman to marry a Christian or any non-Muslim. Muslim men, on the other hand, are allowed to marry non-Muslims, since the expectation is that the father will take control and raise his children Muslim, regardless of the woman's wishes. As in so many other parts of life, Muslim women are considered too weak to do the same. Of course, none of this applied to me at the time, but a step in the wrong direction was noted. The fact that I wore torn jeans and wanted to integrate into the Austrian culture was enough to convince the community that I was a bad influence.

In 1997, at the age of fifteen, I was accepted into an upper-level baccalaureate school that offered advanced academic learning for intellectually gifted students. It specialized in music and acting, which suited me perfectly. Now, instead of wanting to become a doctor, I dreamed of becoming a Bollywood actress. My parents thought this was a phase and that it was best that I get it out of my system while I was still in the protective environment of school. All that mattered to them was that I get a diploma to be impressive for my future husband's family and that I stay out of trouble.

There were more than twenty young people in my grade, mostly Austrian girls who looked a decade older than me because of how they dressed and acted. They wore tight jeans and shorts that emphasized their figures, they had stylish haircuts featuring different colors of the rainbow, they smoked, some of them had piercings on their face, and some even had boyfriends. During breaks they would gossip about parties they had been to over the weekend, about bars they had gone to, about the concerts they wanted to see and the boys they had met, while I just stood there silently, feeling like I had landed from a different planet.

To these city girls, I was doubly naive: I was a sheltered Pakistani girl who prayed regularly and whose only experience of the West had come from living in a tiny country village. I was never going to fit in, nor was I particularly interested in what my classmates were doing. I didn't smoke because I thought it was unfitting for a Pakistani woman, and I didn't want to drink alcohol because that was forbidden to Muslims. And I wasn't interested in boys. What would I do with a boy? The boys in my age group were after only one thing: sex. I wanted no part of that. I believed sex before marriage was deeply immoral. But when I said this to the girls in my class, they simply laughed at me. I never went to parties, didn't go to any bars, and never even considered going to a concert because my parents would have not allowed such a thing. I didn't yet dare to question my parents' Islamic rules, and as a result, I was an outcast at school.

I was convinced that I was right and that my classmates were wrong, but I was very lonely in my convictions and there was no one I could talk with about it. I felt outnumbered. My sister Aisha was only ten years old, and her interests didn't extend beyond her dolls. And my mother was definitely the wrong person. I didn't need to ask her to know what she thought about the girls in my class. In her opinion they were spoiled brats who had absolutely no sense of decency or honor. They dressed in shorts and thought like prostitutes; they were unclean and would burn in Hell. The only other women in my life were my mother's friends, and all these women were Pakistani — they all thought, lived, and felt exactly as my mother did.

The longer I lived in Linz, the more uncertain I became about the demands of my mother. I accepted her role as a housewife and mother as the only option for a woman. I never questioned that for a moment. But did I really want to live like her? Yes, I wanted to get married someday and have children, but I still wanted to be free to make a choice.

I constantly thought about my role as an outsider. Where did I belong? At home I was considered to be not religious enough and at school everyone thought I was too religious. I was drawn to the freedom of having a free will. I had been in Austria for five years and, unlike my mother, I loved my life here. But I wanted it to be *my* life, with choices that I had made. I'd become westernized — without even noticing it. The great loneliness I was suffering started to have an impact on my performance at school. My parents were horrified: I had always been one of the best in the class and now I was having problems in every subject. They asked me what was wrong, but I couldn't tell them what was tormenting me. They'd never understand.

I started to dress in two layers: first the sleeveless top that I wanted to wear at school and over that the blouse my mother approved of. On the street I took off the blouse and stuffed it into my schoolbag until the afternoon when I took it out again, pulled it over my head, and went home. My masquerade worked for a few months. When I got on the tram, I was dressed just like all the other girls, and by the time I got to school I was just like other teenagers. I no longer had problems with any of my classmates. I stood around with them during the breaks, complained about the teachers, and listened excitedly when they talked about how they had spent their weekends. Although I still had very little to contribute to their reports on kissing and hooking up, I had the feeling that I had finally been accepted at school. Being happy made my school marks improve as well.

I was leading a real double life. Luckily, my mother couldn't read my thoughts — or the diary in which I wrote down those thoughts and which I kept hidden so securely that she would never find it. It was just a tiny bit of freedom, a freedom that every Christian teenage girl has without even thinking about it, but that I fought for with my tricks. I thought it was fantastic to have friends again, even if they were Christians. Although I couldn't go to the movies or birthday parties with my friends, I stood around with them during breaks at school.

But gradually my mother noticed the change and became increasingly suspicious. Farah's family made comments about my appearance to her. Her father told my mother that he saw me in town speaking with boys. My mother began to spy on me, watching me through the kitchen window to see what I was wearing when I got off the tram. If she saw that I wasn't dressed like a Muslim girl, there were endless scoldings.

In Sarleinsbach, she had never cared how I spent my afternoons. There I could have spent the entire afternoon running through the gardens and fields with no objections on her part. But the older I got, the stricter and more distrustful she became. This was one of the main reasons for her concern — I had started my period. In Pakistan, this meant that I was a woman, with everything that entailed. Of course, I had no idea what was happening to me. In most Muslim families, matters related to a woman's body are not discussed openly. The day my period started, my mother was in the hospital undergoing major surgery. Everything at home was entrusted to me, including making dinner and caring for my siblings. I didn't know why I was bleeding. I ran to my neighbor's house in tears, thinking that I was sick. She laughed and said, "You have become a woman." I had no idea what that meant. But she gave me a pad. I put it on the wrong way and cried in my room because it wasn't working. Meanwhile my mother cried in the hospital when my father told her that I hadn't prepared dinner. She thought that she had failed in raising a good daughter.

Once I "became a woman," my parents began enforcing strict Islamic rules, in preparation for my future husband. That meant spending virtually all my time at home. There is a Pakistani saying, "A girl is a burden on the shoulder of her father until she is married," and my mother repeated it frequently. Whenever I behaved inappropriately — in a non-Muslim way — she told me off and called me *haram di kutti* (impure dog). In her opinion, I often behaved inappropriately, not merely to provoke her but out of conviction. I had fought for so long to integrate into Western culture. And the longer I lived in Austria, and in Linz in particular, the clearer it became to me how I imagined my future: I wanted to stay here, to live here — in the same way everybody else did. I wanted my life to be here, not back in Pakistan. Although I loved my country, it felt a million miles away and thousands of years in the past.

My mother had a completely different view. She repeatedly urged me not to give myself over so much to Austria, where there were only "sinners" and "unbelievers." She said that our real life was in Pakistan, In my parents' eyes, I was a Pakistani girl, and this issue wasn't up for discussion. They were convinced that we would eventually return to Pakistan. They were becoming more Pakistani even though we were so far away.

Perhaps it was because I had grown up in Austria, but it was clear to me that I wanted to be completely different from my mother. I wanted to study, to earn my own money, and someday marry a man whom I had chosen myself. I didn't want a life someone else had chosen for me. I was rejecting my parents' Islamic tradition in favor of my own independence. I didn't realize this at the time. All I wanted was a little freedom — to go outside by myself and meet my girlfriends, to make my own decisions. I could not see how these things were wrong. In Christian families, parents encourage their children to be independent, but in the Muslim world an independent woman is a dishonorable woman. An honorable woman is first obedient to her parents and their choices for her, and after her marriage obedient to her husband and his choices for her.

My father also started to impose new rules on a regular basis. When I asked him if it would be okay to join a basketball class, he refused. I went there anyway, until he showed up and made a scene. "You are a woman," he would repeat constantly, and that meant numerous, strict prohibitions. I had to go straight home after school. And when my girlfriends met up over the summer to go swimming, I definitely wasn't allowed to go with them.

Still, I carried on with my game of hide-and-seek. I prayed to please Allah and tried to keep as many of his rules as I could, so that the weight of my scale would be heavy with good deeds, but on the other hand were the Austrians who were expecting me to integrate into the country where I lived. It was extremely strenuous to switch back and forth like this. My mother checked everything. Sometimes she even took my schoolbag away from me when I came home from school.

The stress was unbearable, and I didn't know what to do. Sometimes I would break down and cry in the middle of class. My teacher, who knew little about Islamic culture, accused me of being nothing more than an attention-seeker. She thought I was just making up a story to get out of class, like other children did.

Meanwhile, the prohibitions grew ever stricter — and more absurd. They dominated every part of my life. I liked the theater and had signed up for the school's drama class. My teacher said I had talent, and I pursued my new hobby with passion. We rehearsed once a week, and with each rehearsal my enthusiasm grew. Until my father found out. In his opinion, theater was something for "prostitutes" and "infidel women" — in other words, not for me. He forbade me to attend any further rehearsals. He said that I was "a disgrace to the family." I didn't understand how it was that he could sit and watch Bollywood movies with me, if all actors were prostitutes. But I had to stop attending the drama class.

I was scared for my future. I filled up the pages of my diary and prayed to Allah to persuade my parents to let me do more. Yet nothing changed.

4

Running Away

My life at school eventually started to improve when I found a boyfriend. Little did I know that this tiny development, so exhilarating at the time, would trigger the familial breakdown that would end in me fleeing home entirely.

It all began when I started spending more time in the school's computer lab. I was looking for pen pals in the United States and England to practice my English. As it happened, there were also some English speakers at our school — exchange students from the United States. One of them was a boy called Bekim. He was an American Muslim with Albanian roots but had grown up in North Carolina with his parents. The other, Immanuel, was a black Christian boy from the Bronx. Bekim was a year older than I was and good looking. All the girls in my circle thought he was cute, and I think he knew this. He dressed like the rappers I saw on MTV and lounged around in front of the school after class or played basketball with Immanuel. I liked him, but only from a distance.

Our paths crossed often enough, but it still took a very long time before we spoke to each other. I didn't want to speak to him first, and he obviously didn't have the nerve to approach me. One day I met the two boys in the Internet room. I sat down at one of the computers and opened my email. Overnight I had received a couple of emails from my pen pals and one from somebody I didn't know. I opened it.

"You look sexy today," was all it said. Who was this unknown sender? Who was calling me sexy? I turned around to see the grinning faces of the two boys.

"Did you send this email?" I asked.

The two flooded my email address, but it soon became clear who I was interested in. Bekim was Muslim, and we started going off on our own.

I was sixteen, a teenage girl in Linz, and suddenly I had my first boyfriend. It was wonderful. Bekim and I sat together for hours on end and talked. We usually met during breaks at school or in the afternoons. We did what any teenage couple does — sometimes we went for walks or played basketball together, but usually we just sat in the park next to the school talking. As we played basketball, we listened to Snoop Dogg, and Bekim helped me memorize the lyrics to Eminem and Dr. Dre songs. But we rarely went out in public, and never on a date: I was terrified of being seen with him by one of my parents' acquaintances, even though Bekim was a Muslim.

Our relationship never went much farther than a kiss. I even felt guilt about kissing him, as I knew my parents would die of shame, but on the other hand, he was a Muslim and therefore I told myself that Allah could not object. I learned later that Islam forbids women even to spend time with, hold hands, or kiss a man to whom they are not married. Our relationship continued for about a month, and I was happy. My heart raced when I saw Bekim, and I almost died of embarrassment when I took his hand because my palms were soaking wet. I filled pages of my diary writing rapturously about him. He told me I was his dream woman and constantly took pictures because he thought I was beautiful. It made me proud, not least because he was one of the most popular boys in school.

One day, at the beginning of March 1998, I came home after meeting Bekim, having told my parents that I had an extra class. Smiling, I got out of the elevator and rang our doorbell. My parents had never given me my own key, so that they could keep an eye on me better. My sister opened the door and looked at me gloomily.

"What's wrong, Aisha?" I asked.

"Nothing," she said and ran into our room.

I followed her and then I saw it: My diary lay on the floor with the pages torn out and scattered around the entire room. At that moment my mother came into the room. Even before I could say hello she started hitting me. Her right hand cracked across my left cheek.

"Who do you think you are?" she screamed. "You're a whore!"

She grabbed my hair, dragged me through the room, and slammed me against the wall. Again and again, she tore at my hair, punched me in the face, and kicked me. I cried and screamed but my mother didn't stop. She kept on shouting that I was a disgrace to the family, an "Austrian whore." My sister tried to squeeze herself between us, but my mother just pushed her aside. I tried to explain that it wasn't serious between Bekim and me, but she just didn't want to listen.

"You can't do that. You're promised to somebody in Pakistan."

At first, I thought I hadn't heard her correctly.

"You're promised to someone. So, behave yourself," she repeated.

I was horrified. My parents had already hinted a few times that they had shortly after my birth arranged my wedding in Pakistan. I had heard this without really taking it seriously. When I was still small, they always told me that one day I would marry Salman, the son of my mother's sister. Salman was my age and lived with his parents in Lahore. In Pakistan I hadn't seen him often, perhaps only two or three times. I remembered him as a very quiet, reserved boy. In any event, I hadn't taken their hints seriously then — and in Austria I had forgotten about them completely.

My mother calmed down after a few minutes. I sat on the bed crying, with my little sister beside me, also in tears. When my father came home that evening, he and my mother called me into the living room. He was surprisingly nice. I had to apologize to him and promise never to meet with a boy again. I promised him. I half believed it myself.

"I forgive you," he said. "But it must never happen again!"

My teacher at the time had once told me that I could always talk to him if I had problems. Now I had one, but did I really want to go to him? Then everything would be official. I didn't want to harm my mother and father; they were my parents, after all. On the other hand, what if it happened again? What if my mother hit me so brutally again? All morning, I could barely concentrate in class. Should I talk to him, or was it better not to?

I chose to move forward. We went where nobody could hear us. He noticed immediately how difficult it was for me to tell him everything — and assured me of his confidence. So I told him the whole story. He listened patiently, then disappeared briefly into the conference room and came back with a brochure for a shelter. He said that I should talk to these people and that they could help me.

When I left the school that day, I thought long and hard about what I should do. Should I really go to the shelter? I didn't know what to expect there, and I also thought it would be a pretty big step to take. True, my mother had hit me hard, but she was also my mother. She was Pakistani and could hardly speak a word of German. What if the staff at the shelter were to create problems for her? It was clear to me that there was no way out of my situation. I wasn't like my parents, that much was clear. Nor did I want to live the kind of life that they had planned for me — and I certainly didn't want to marry Salman. I didn't want to have a big fight with my parents, but it was clear that, given my problems, a confrontation was inevitable sooner or later. I felt Austrian, but they lived by the moral values of Islam.

Seeking advice, I went to the shelter. The people there were kind and promised to take me in and protect me if I needed it. I felt reassured, and afterward I went home. My mother, who was completely out of control the day before, hardly paid any attention to me, even though I was almost two hours late. I was a little surprised by this, but also relieved. Perhaps she regretted what had happened the day before; perhaps everything would be better now.

But nothing improved — absolutely nothing. My mother managed to control herself for exactly one week and then everything was the same as before, only worse. She didn't allow me any freedom at all. I wasn't allowed to meet my girlfriends or go to the cinema in the afternoon, not even to the matinees. She hit me for the smallest thing. Once, while we were sitting in our dining room, she took a glass bottle and smashed it on my head. My father was shocked, but he quickly saw that I was not seriously hurt. Even so, I cried and shielded my bruised head while he defended me. In the afternoon when I came home, my mother was standing at the kitchen window to see who I got off the tram with. Sometimes it was enough if Pakistani friends told my parents something. If they saw me in town after school with friends, there was a big fight at home, and if they were male friends, I got hit even harder.

It went on like this for almost a year. I was living in a prison in the middle of Linz. I developed bulimia. My brothers weren't particularly interested in my struggle. They were two and four years younger than me and had the freedom I'd wanted. They could do whatever they liked after school. They went to parties and soccer matches with their Bosnian friends. My sister was on my side, but since she was only ten years old, she was still too young to understand. All she knew is that I was often sad and cried constantly at night. My father was somewhat friendlier than my mother, but you couldn't have described him as liberal.

Every day I felt with increasing clarity the differences between my world and that of my parents. Unlike them, I grew up in a relatively wealthy, individualistic country where there were different standards for human dignity. Teachers were not allowed to beat children, everybody could go to a decent school, and there were far more options for women than the narrow prospect of marrying a cousin. My parents started to talk constantly about my future wedding in Pakistan, and they told me about my cousin Salman — how good-looking he was, what an excellent student he was, and what a nice man he had turned into. Like me, the last time they had seen Salman was six years before. They tried to convince me that I'd be happy with him and pressured me to conform to their way of life.

The more they insisted, the more they reached back to Pakistan. My parents often phoned my grandfather's family, and my mother spoke regularly to her sister, Salman's mother. One evening, just as I was doing my homework, I heard my mother on the phone with her sister. I tried to eavesdrop, but she was talking too quietly. All I could hear through the closed door was her repeatedly expressing her thanks. After she hung up, she came into my room, and I saw that she had tears in her eyes. They were tears of joy. She came up to me and hugged me for the first time in months.

"She has accepted you. Your aunt wants you to be her daughter-in-law," she said.

Tears sprang into my eyes too — although certainly not tears of happiness. I was sixteen and there were plenty of things I still wanted to do with my life. Marrying my cousin and living locked up in a village somewhere in Pakistan was definitely not one of them. I was so furious that I said exactly that to my mother, earning me a worse beating than ever before.

In the following weeks the abuse became even worse. Hardly any time passed without my mother hitting me. By February, I had had enough and went back to the shelter. Two social workers were directly in charge of my case. I told them everything, including their plans for me to marry Salman, whereupon they decided we should all have a family talk. Although they had tried very hard to understand my problems, they just couldn't pierce through the deep-rooted cultural differences.

This meeting between the social workers, my parents, and me took place the next day, February 25, 1999, at the shelter. It was a disaster. As I entered the conference room, my father glared at me with reproach.

My mother called me a stupid pig. My father tried to calm her down, and I tried to avoid his eyes. I felt guilty — I had disappointed him, disappointed my community, disappointed Allah.

My parents denied everything: I had never been hit and allegedly I had every freedom one could imagine. They told the social workers that even the arranged marriage was much less dramatic than I had described it. My father assured them that if I married Salman, it would be by my choice. The social workers noted everything and wrote in the official report: "The parents appear to be very cooperative. On the other hand, their religious-cultural values were made very clear." My parents and I returned home.

My relationship with Bekim ended. First, he stopped sending me nice emails and began to distance himself, finding excuses for why he couldn't meet me after school as we usually did. I finally confronted him in the schoolyard one day and asked him if he had stopped liking me.

"No, but you Pakistanis are strange people. Just go marry your cousin, Sabatina," he said. We never spoke again and avoided each other at school. I'd always known we didn't have a future anyway — he would have to go back to the United States, and I could never leave my family. I let him know I was angry, though: I wrote him a letter using all the insults and curse words in the rap songs he'd taught me.

At home, it became clear that something awful would soon happen, but I had resigned myself to it. When it finally did happen one day in May, the reason for the escalation was negligible: a T-shirt that my mother had found in the linen basket and deemed too revealing. In the same way that I wasn't wearing makeup just to look pretty, she wasn't beating me over a T-shirt. It was everything that T-shirt represented — everything I had come to represent.

I was still in my pajamas when my mother's yelling started. I could already hear her shouting in the bathroom and then she appeared in my room with the T-shirt in her hand, a far-from-scandalous shirt with short sleeves. She took the T-shirt and smacked me around the head with it. I burst into tears and shouted back that she should stop when, in her rage, she grabbed a pointed shoe and walloped me with all her strength in the face. I felt my lip bursting open. Blood trickled out of my mouth. I staggered out of the apartment, still in my pajamas. It was just a reflexive action, but I simply couldn't bear her beatings anymore.

I ran downstairs as fast as I could and rang the doorbell of the first apartment I came to. A young African woman, whom I had seen a few times but had never spoken to, lived there. Luckily, she was at home. She opened the door and gave me a shocked look. I must have been a terrible sight to see — barefoot, wearing pajamas, and smeared with blood. Without a word she pulled me into the apartment and closed the door behind me. Her name was Nira; she was twenty years old and came from Ghana.

"I don't want my mother to find me. Please hide me," I pleaded.

"Sit down first and tell me what's wrong," she replied.

Nira was tall and had a warm, friendly face. She worked as a hairdresser in Linz. Although I had only seen her around, I still trusted her. She listened attentively to me and agreed to help.

We stayed holed up in her apartment the whole day. Nira didn't want my mother to be able to see us from the kitchen window, so we waited until it was dark. She lent me a pair of jeans, a sweatshirt, and shoes and, once we were certain that nobody could see us, we left the house. On May 12, 1999, I moved into the youth homeless shelter.

The social workers were kind to me, and I had the impression that they had all firmly expected that I would show up on their doorstep at some point. I settled in, preparing to stay for an extended period. Each day, I went from there to school and tried to continue my life in as normal a fashion as possible. My parents repeatedly called the shelter to try to persuade me to come home, but I stayed put. I heard that my grandfather had called my father and ordered him to make me see reason; otherwise the family's honor would be lost and I would bring great shame on everybody. I was terribly afraid of the repercussions from my parents and their Pakistani friends.

My family didn't give up. They called again and again, threatening the counselors, saying that I had to come home immediately or they would disown me. The elder of my two brothers also called and abused me so loudly on the phone that one of the counselors took the receiver out of my hand and simply hung up.

While I was there, I tried calling Razia, because I thought she and her liberal Muslim parents could make mine see reason. I trusted and looked up to Razia because she had a very Western outlook, and I thought she might be able to understand my problem. But my call with her made clear the whole Muslim community had closed itself off.

"Please leave us in peace and don't bother us with your problems!" she said and hung up the phone.

A couple of days later, my parents arrived at the shelter unannounced. Once again, we had a meeting with the social workers. My father promised me that everything would be all right and my mother too assured me that she would never hit me again. They told the counselors that they would accept my way of life and that I could do whatever I wanted.

Initially, the social workers were skeptical, but slowly they began to trust my parents. Islam allows you to lie to non-Muslims for the sake of spreading the religion. My father appeared very Western, and he promised the social workers that I would be given all the freedom I wanted. My parents can be very charming and loving when they choose, and the social workers allowed themselves to be persuaded by their performance.

That was one of the challenges I faced when speaking about the abuse. Whenever people saw my father or brothers, they acted as if they were in the presence of gods. One of my friends even said, "I don't know what your parents do or don't do, but I saw your father, and he is one handsome, beautiful man."

When I brought up in conversation that I was concerned that my parents would send me to Pakistan to get married, my father laughed it off innocently! The social workers could not believe that my parents would be so cruel as to force me into marriage. I found it very difficult to explain that my father might just be playing a role in order to take me home and save face in the community. I knew I wasn't being taken seriously. The social workers had told me earlier that my parents had the right to call the police to take me home because I was a minor. They urged me to go home with my parents and said they were sure nothing would happen. What choice did I have? I was trapped by my culture. On May 20, 1999, I went home with my parents.

Surprisingly, the situation actually did change completely this time. My parents were friendly and suddenly there was no more drama when I came home two hours after school had ended. Even my mother was kinder to me.

I would learn why only a week later. My father came home from work earlier than usual. He asked me to come into the kitchen and told me that he had an idea for how we could ensure that everything would get better.

"We're going back to Pakistan," he announced. "And there you can do whatever you want."

"Whatever I want?" I asked.

"Yes," he replied. "You can go to drama school or take singing lessons. But come back with us to Pakistan. Everything is better there."

Strange as it may sound, I trusted them. I wanted to go to drama school, and I thought that since Pakistan is a Muslim country, they wouldn't be afraid that the unbelievers were going to lead me astray. To be on the safe side, I spoke to my counselors at the shelter, and they had no objections. They even said that it might do me good to visit my home country again. Perhaps, they said, my parents would finally realize that I didn't fit in there because I had changed so much, and then all our problems would be solved. Their arguments persuaded me, and I agreed. But then I learned there was one condition attached to this plan.

"When you go back," my father said, "You must get engaged to your cousin Salman. Then your grandfather's honor as head of the family — and mine with regard to Salman's mother — is restored."

"After all, you've been promised to Salman since your birth," my mother said.

I paused for a moment before I started screaming.

"I won't marry Salman. I don't want to marry anyone at all, at least not yet. And why does everything revolve around this family honor?"

"Because it's the most important thing. Much more important than you," my mother replied.

My eyes filled with tears. I stood up from the table and stormed off to my room. My father followed me and sat down on the edge of my bed.

"Sabatina," he said. "Think about it. Pakistan really is better for you. You can be an actress there and you don't have to marry Salman. You just need to get engaged and then everything will be all right."

Compared with all the other things I had been through with my family, this condition didn't seem so bad. I was still only sixteen years old, and I couldn't manage breaking up with my family forever. I wasn't prepared to bring shame on my family, especially on my father. And anyway, hadn't the social workers said that I would be safe in Pakistan?

Now, with the benefit of hindsight, I know that the social workers fatally misjudged the situation. They had no concept of how Muslim culture really works, and it very nearly cost me my life. But in that moment, when my father hugged me — his smile full of promises — I felt truly happy.

I would see Pakistan again. I would see my cousins again. Maybe I could become an actress. I didn't think about my engagement to Salman at all.

5

THE ENGAGEMENT

MY FIRST HOURS in Pakistan are a pleasant memory. I was excited to
be going back to visit my friends and relatives, excited that my parents
had said they would let me attend acting school if I wanted, excited to
feel all the attention that was turned toward me when we first arrived.
Only later did I realize why everyone was being so pleasant, and what
this trip would really ask of me. What started out as a family holiday
turned into a long prison sentence, designed to break my spirit.

We left for Pakistan on the first day of the summer holidays in 1999.
My father had taken a five-week holiday and wanted to spend all of
it in Pakistan. Ahmed, my father's friend from Sarleinsbach who had
collected us from the airport almost seven years before, came to the
house to drive us back. We were all excited. In the weeks leading up
to our trip, my mother had talked constantly about her siblings. My
brothers were looking forward to playing soccer and cricket with their
Pakistani cousins again and my father wanted to show his own father
how well his family had turned out — hopefully, he could obscure
my willful behavior and show a happy, united family to his father. My
sister was the most delighted of all. She was very young when we left
Pakistan, and she had no memories of her life there; she had no idea
what to expect in Lahore and Dhadar.

Even I was looking forward to the trip. I was curious about my
old home, my relatives, and my friends. For years I hadn't heard from
them and asked myself how they had turned out. The real reason for

our trip — my engagement to Salman — I completely pushed out of my mind. I was sure that it would never happen if I didn't want it to. When I said goodbye to my friends in Linz, it was as if I was simply going on a long holiday. I promised to keep in touch and send them postcards, but I couldn't say how long we would be staying. I knew that my father had a five-week holiday, but if I liked it in Pakistan and really could go to an acting school then I would stay there; if not, then I would return to Linz in the autumn and continue my education. As far as I was concerned, it was as simple as that. My parents' wishes, my pending engagement, the distance between Pakistan and Linz — I successfully blocked them from my mind.

It was well past midnight when we arrived in Lahore. The moment we stepped off the plane to get into the shuttle bus, Pakistan welcomed me with a hot blast of air. I gasped for breath, unable to breathe in the heat that permeated even the darkest hours of night. It was hot and stuffy and there was a thick haze of humidity hanging over the city. When we reached the arrivals hall, I saw the reason for our trip. I recognized him immediately, even though we hadn't seen each other for many years. He was waiting there with his father: Salman, my cousin — and, according to the will of my parents, my future husband.

First, he greeted my parents and my siblings, and then he approached me. He had grown, as I'm sure I had as well, and although he was two months younger than I was, he was at least a head taller. He also had dark hair and dark eyes like his father, and he was well-dressed in Western attire. It was clear that he wasn't quite sure how he should greet me. He knew why we were here and that I was his future wife, but he hardly knew me. Should he hug me in the same friendly way as he hugged my brothers? That would be unthinkable in Pakistan. He decided to just greet me and smile.

"I am happy that you're here. I have often dreamed about you," he said so quietly that only I could hear him.

I took a step backward.

"Salman bhai, it is mutual," I responded loudly.

I wanted to be nice to him but at the same time make it clear to him where we stood. All male relatives of one's own age are addressed in Pakistani with *bhai*, or brother. I hoped that he understood what I meant by using the term. Still, I felt that his meeting us at the airport couldn't be a good omen.

Salman and his father helped us with the luggage before we went out to the large parking garage in front of the airport where it was even hotter than on the runway. There wasn't the slightest breeze. My sister sighed loudly. "Is it always this hot here?" she asked, and my brothers and I started laughing.

We loaded the luggage into a large car, a Suzuki pickup that my uncle had borrowed from his neighbor. Then we set off for the Gulshan Ali Colony, the district of Lahore where Salman and his family lived. On the way, memories of my childhood were awakened: The air was filled with the stench of gas and refuse and overlaid with the intense smell of curry. Even though it was late at night, there were cars and people everywhere. People were driving in every direction — cars, buses, bicycles, and innumerable rickshaws. There were no rules of the road here at all — or if there were, nobody was observing them. Nevertheless, I liked the vibrancy and movement of the city, and I liked the feeling of being there again. Perhaps my parents were right when they said everything would be better in Pakistan.

Despite how late it was, when we arrived at my uncle's house, I saw that our relatives had prepared a huge reception for us. My uncle had barely parked the car when the door opened and my aunt, my cousins, and neighbors flooded out. They were at least as curious and as excited as we were.

As we got out of the car, my aunt ran toward us, hugging and kissing us extravagantly, me in particular. For a moment I was worried that she wasn't going to let go of me. She looked deep into my eyes.

"Everything will be all right now," she whispered.

I couldn't figure out what she meant — but I didn't like the sound of it. Once we had gone into the house, my aunt hardly moved from my side. She was especially friendly and obliging, bringing me chai and biscuits and taking care of me in a touching fashion. She asked me endless questions about what it was like in Austria, whether I liked it there, whether I enjoyed going to school. She even wanted to know everything about my girlfriends. And she wasn't the only one: Everyone was paying attention to me. It was very strange. I had never been the center of attention in my family. Unlike my brothers, the sons and heirs, I was almost incidental.

I couldn't say I wasn't a little pleased by all the attention. In Linz, I could never please my parents, I was always doing something wrong. Here, I was fussed over and everybody listened to me when I had something to say — everybody, that is, except Salman, who appeared at first to be ignoring me. He stood against the wall the whole time and acted as if he had no interest in me whatsoever. Nevertheless, I couldn't fail to notice that he didn't take his eyes off me once. "I hope he's not getting his hopes up," I thought to myself as I went over and tried to chat with him. I asked him how he was, what school he was going to, and what hobbies he had, but he just gave me evasive answers, staring at me all the while.

Finally, I pulled a photo out of my bag that showed all my school-mates and started to explain to him in detail who all these people were and which ones were my friends. He didn't seem particularly interested in my descriptions, but I hoped that he understood my hint. I wanted him to see that these people were in my life and that I liked them, hoping that he would reject me from the beginning for being too westernized.

We stayed with Salman's parents in Lahore for just under a week. It was exactly like it used to be: the men left the house early to take care of various things while we women remained at home. It was unbearable, but it seemed like there was no escape. I felt trapped because I was. I looked Pakistani, I spoke Urdu, and I was now in Pakistan for an extended period of time. But I knew that that wasn't really who I was — I wasn't a completely Pakistani girl and never would be.

The longer we spent in Pakistan, the clearer this became, especially once we went back to Dhadar. As we passed the first houses in my hometown, I noticed how tense my father was. I understand the pressure he was under. He had always loved Dhadar, possibly because he left when he was about eighteen to go to Europe. For my father, Dhadar was something very special, a place where, above all, he was given respect — largely owing to my grandfather's position.

While my father always remained a foreigner in Europe, never living in the best neighborhoods and not speaking the language perfectly, here he was highly respected. Whenever he came home, the neighbors insisted on hearing his stories from abroad, and when he voiced an opinion, it carried weight. Perhaps that explains why respect, and the family's reputation in particular, was so important to my father: Once he had it, he was unwilling to lose it, at any cost.

We stayed in Dhadar for a week, and I felt uneasy there from the first moment. In Lahore, it had been bad enough having to sit around the house all the time, but in Dhadar, it was completely intolerable. After all, Dhadar was the village where I knew most of the people. Why should I be afraid just because I might run into someone from my childhood on the street? As a little girl I used to run around the village with my girlfriends for hours on end; I knew every corner, every tree, and every well. Why was this activity now prohibited? Only because I was six years older and had gotten my period?

I equally failed to understand the way my cousins reacted to these restrictions. I had the impression that they had accepted their fates and had turned into silent, blindly obedient women. They wore the salwar kameez, spoke only when spoken to, and did nothing but take care of the household. I tried to talk to them a few times, but in vain. When I told them about school, they simply shook their heads disbelievingly.

How was it possible that boys and girls could be in the same class? They had no idea about the films I had seen or the books I had read. They had no idea about life in the West and acted as if they didn't want to know either. It was similar the other way around. They told me about their recipes and talked about the latest village gossip, which didn't interest me in the slightest.

But nothing could have prepared me for the visit of my childhood friend, Deira. Although I was overjoyed at first, I knew the moment Deira walked into the house that nothing was the way it had been before. As children, we had been closer than sisters. We shared every secret and every laugh. When I left for Austria, I knew that nothing could come between us; I knew that our friendship was stronger than distance. When Deira came over, she wore a long white salwar kameez and had her hair concealed under a veil. But that wasn't the biggest shock: My Deira had turned into a silent, reserved woman. She sat on the living room couch, taking care not to make any inappropriate movements and to appear unobtrusive, as if she didn't exist at all. We talked about my life in Austria, but with every sentence I saw more clearly how disturbed she was by my stories. She was scandalized when I told her that women could sit in a café and chat there with boys, as I had done in Linz. And when I told her that in the summer, I sometimes went to the swimming pool, she looked as shocked as if I had confided that I went to bed with a different boy every day.

The only diversion she had had in the last seven years had been two visits to Lahore, where she went with her family to do some shopping. Her life was played out within a household of roughly five hundred square feet and a courtyard of just over a thousand square feet, yet this didn't seem to bother her at all. She told me that she would be getting married the following year — naturally, to a man she had never seen before — and was looking forward to it: to the wedding, to her husband, and to the children he would give her.

I was deeply shaken when she left. It was obvious to me that Deira had developed in the only way she could in this environment. She had become a well-behaved Muslim woman who didn't need to think about her future because it had all been decided for her. I was sorry for her because I felt that her life was over before it had really begun. And at the same time, seeing Deira shocked me because it so clearly illustrated to me, as never before in Pakistan, how my parents wanted me to be.

But I wasn't like that. I still had my life ahead of me. Of that I was certain. To this day, I have never again seen nor heard from Deira, but it is safe to assume that she lives the life of any other woman in Dhadar: bearing children, raising them, keeping house, and keeping quiet.

The days in Dhadar passed, each day the same as the one before, the same as the ones before we came, the same as the days had passed when we'd lived there years before. We got up and had our breakfast of flatbread and chai before the men left the house. The women cooked, cleaned, and chatted. When they ran out of things to talk about, previous subjects were recycled and rehashed. It was horrific. I wasn't allowed to leave the house and, unfortunately, I had nothing much to say to my aunts or cousins.

A constant theme of conversation during my stay was my impending engagement to Salman, about which most of my relatives naturally knew, as did my cousins, who regularly asked me about him. They wanted to know what it was like with him and whether I was already looking forward to the wedding. For them, I was the lucky one — no doubt about it. They all knew Salman and thought he was clever and handsome.

"You really got lucky," my cousin Laila said.

When I burst into derisive laughter, she looked at me in astonishment. She herself was promised to a distant relative whom she had never seen. But this didn't bother her. In fact, she was looking forward to her wedding because it meant that she would leave Dhadar to move to a different village and start a new life. It was deeply irritating to her that I didn't value my engagement to Salman and even laughed about it. She couldn't believe that in Austria nobody marries someone they don't know just because their parents insist on it, and that I couldn't see myself in that situation. Our conversation came to a rapid end when I saw that I wouldn't be able to convince Laila, and she wouldn't be able to convince me.

Only a day later, however, my father and grandfather summoned me. They were furious. At first, I couldn't figure out why, but when they mentioned my conversation with Laila I understood. I had hurt and upset them.

"Who do you think you are?" screamed my father. "How can you dishonor your family with such stories?"

I started crying. "I don't mean to dishonor you, but I don't want to marry Salman."

"You will marry him. You will not dishonor your father and mother," commanded my grandfather, enraged while he held a sickle under my throat.

I was scared to death and realized that I was trapped. My parents had lied to me at the shelter when they said if I came to Pakistan I could "do what I wanted." I was in Pakistan, in a place where I could be sure that nobody would help me. There was no emergency shelter here, no social worker to whom I could flee. What could I do if they forced me into marriage? I could have kicked myself. How could I have been so stupid to trust them, to come to their home and hand myself over to this society? Nevertheless, I still had a tiny glimmer of hope that we would be returning to Austria soon. After all, we had already been here for more than three weeks, which meant that my father would have to start work again soon. That would be the end of this torture.

I was relieved when I heard that we would be returning to Lahore. That could mean only that we would be flying back to Austria within a few days. I had already told my parents that I didn't want to stay there because it obviously wasn't going to work out with acting school. Since they didn't respond to this, I assumed that they had accepted my decision.

What I didn't realize was that while I was trying to reason with them as a westernized teenage girl, they were as Muslim as ever. No amount of compromise or discussion would get me what I wanted — they were my parents, and they would do what was best for the family's honor. Their silence wasn't an acknowledgement of my rights, but a deaf ear to their disobedient daughter.

When we arrived at my uncle and aunt's house, I was at first surprised that so many relatives had gathered there. My grandfather had traveled from Dhadar, as had my uncles, aunts, and cousins. The significance should have been clear to me at that moment, but I was still in denial. All afternoon I sat in the courtyard with my cousins and told them how much I was looking forward to going back to Austria. Toward evening, my uncle, Salman's father, came out and asked me to come with him into the living room. And there they all sat in a semicircle around my grandfather: my father, my mother, Salman's mother, two other aunts and uncles, and Salman himself, whose usual indifferent expression was tinged with tension.

The room was decorated with flowers and the walls were covered in pictures and photos of family members. An intense smell of curry and flowers filled the room. In that moment I could no longer hide from it all; repressing it wouldn't help. So many relatives had shown up because it was here and now that my future would be decided — and in a way that I wouldn't have imagined, even in my worst nightmares.

For a long time, there was an ominous silence in the room. Everyone stared at me and Salman. Finally, my aunt spoke.

"We have just decided that you are to be my daughter-in-law."

My aunt meant it seriously and I saw that she was pleased. More than that: She was overjoyed. Her eyes shone like they had never shone before, at least not since I had been in Lahore. I looked around me.

Everybody was trying to look as solemn as possible. What was I supposed to do? There was no doubt that they were serious. But I couldn't run away; there was nobody who would help me. I gulped and decided to turn the whole thing into a joke.

"Hey, Salman bhai, did you hear them? You're going to change from being my brother to being my husband. Isn't that great?"

"Stop this nonsense immediately! This is not a joking matter," snarled my mother, who had stood up. I had never seen her so furious. A deep frown of rage was carved above the bridge of her nose, and a blue-colored vein was beating at her temple. "You will marry Salman and that's that!" she shouted, so loud that her voice broke.

"No! Never!" Now my voice cracked as well. I was angrier than I had ever been in my life.

At that moment the room broke out in chaos. My mother screamed, all my aunts started talking at the same time, and my father simply repeated over and over: "Shame, shame, this can't be happening."

Until then, my grandfather hadn't said a word and had observed the scene impassively. Now he stood up. Immediately, a deathly calm reigned over the room.

"Haven't you taught this girl any manners?"

Saying this, he walked past me without even deigning to look at me. I felt his trousers touch my leg as he left the room. I had never felt so much coldness in a single person. The other men followed him, while I remained behind with the women.

Immediately, the room became loud again. Everybody talked at the same time, and the words "shame" and "ungrateful child" reached my ears. Coming slowly toward me, my mother started crying with rage. I knew what that meant. I was sweating all over and I felt my face going bright red. I was more terrified than I had been at any of her other outbursts. When my mother was standing in front of me, I saw red patches on her cheeks. Her eyelids were trembling, and I saw that she was breathing deeply. At that moment, she drew her arm back and hit me straight in the face. My cheeks burned and my eyes filled with tears. I threw my arms up in front of my face, but my mother couldn't be stopped. She punched me again and again with her hands and fists. She tore my hair and kicked me painfully with her pointed shoes.

I cried, I screamed, and I shouted for help although I knew that nobody would help me. I didn't even try to run away because I knew there was no point. Where could I have gone? I stood in the middle of the room, as if paralyzed, and tried to protect my face.

"Mama, stop it! You're hurting my sister."

My sister Aisha had heard me crying, rushed in from the next room, and was trying in vain to drag my mother away from me. She was the only one who took pity on me. Finally, Salman stepped in and pulled my mother off me. Holding on to Aisha tightly, I ran out of the room.

"You slut, you should be happy that you're getting a husband at all!"

Those were the last words I heard from my mother before I slammed the door shut behind me.

I was shocked and humiliated. My own mother had beaten me up and my relatives had stood by and watched without making the slightest effort to help me. How cruel can one's own family be? But this wasn't because they were bad people; rather, they were all simply trying to fulfill Allah's commandments. Beating disobedient women is one of them (Koran, sura 4:34). I cried uncontrollably while my little sister sat beside me, deeply shocked. She was only ten, but she had probably guessed that a similar fate awaited her. She too was already promised to a cousin — Aslam — the son of one of my other aunts.

My brothers, on the other hand, were completely unaffected by the incident. They had no sympathy for me but saw me as a troublemaker. When they came into the courtyard, they didn't see me as their sister, but only as a young Pakistani woman who wouldn't do what was required of her.

There was no trace of my father that evening. He had left the house with my grandfather and disappeared into town. He hadn't been present at the scene my mother had made. Having first humiliated me in front of everyone, she now went on to humiliate herself. Again and again, I heard her screaming and moaning in the living room. "Why does she do this to me? I have given birth to a whore!" she repeated, before starting to self-flagellate.

I knew that there were Pakistanis who whipped themselves when they suffered, and now I was a witness to it — and it was my mother. For hours I could hear her screaming and breast-beating, until all at once the house went deathly silent.

Suddenly my aunt was standing beside me.

"Your mother has collapsed. What have you done to her?"

I went into the living room where the other women had laid my mother on the couch. She was almost motionless. Besides other illnesses she had always had problems with her blood pressure, and now it had all been just too much. We called a doctor.

"She has to drink something and take these tablets," he said. But my mother didn't want to.

"Let me die! I have given birth to a whore," she rasped, at which point the doctor ordered my mother to the hospital.

"What kind of a daughter are you? It's your fault that she's so ill!" accused my aunt.

I had come to the end of my strength. I still didn't feel like I was to blame, though — hadn't I always said that I wouldn't marry Salman? But there was so much enmity, so much hatred on all sides, all directed toward me. Here there was nobody standing up for me, and my friends in Austria were a seventeen-hour flight away. I had no idea what was going to happen.

I went into the kitchen to think it over in silence. I was in Pakistan, with no one willing to help me, but I knew one thing for sure: I wasn't going to marry my cousin. I wanted to live my own life, not the one that others had planned for me. But how could I make that happen? I couldn't turn to my parents; they didn't care about any of that. All they could see was that I wasn't a good daughter. Everything that they had promised me in Linz in front of the social workers was suddenly meaningless. They were furious, aggressive, and ready to do anything to protect the family honor and have me marry Salman.

And in one way, I could understand them. They had grown up in a world with completely different values and simply couldn't understand many of the things that moved and interested me. In their view, I had disgraced them, a disgrace which would remain with them forever. My mother had been embarrassed in front of her sisters, her only family. Her parents had died when she was very young, and her sister had raised her. I had been promised to Salman as a thank-you to my aunt for a debt my mother could never repay. And my father, for whom honor, Islamic morality, and respect were even more important, had stood in front of his own father unable to control his daughter. My father, of all people! The man who had always had to fight for recognition and who hoped that he had achieved it thanks to his success in Europe. I had made him into a disgrace.

Was it possible that I was really to blame for everything? Should I have just conformed? Like all the other women in my family? I realized that there was no way out of my situation. At that moment, my eyes fell on the heavy, flat knife, which my aunt used to chop large pieces of meat. Outside the kitchen I could hear my relatives shouting and complaining. I reached for the knife. Suddenly, Salman came rushing through the door. When he saw me, he threw himself at me, tearing me to the ground and hitting the knife out of my hand. He didn't need to say a word — his horrified look said it all. My eyes filled with tears of rage and desperation.

"Salman, please understand. I don't love you. I'm sorry. I will never marry a man I don't love."

For a Pakistani woman it is of course impossible simply to reject a bridegroom. The opposite applies to a man, who can refuse to marry even if his parents have chosen a wife for him. This had happened to a female cousin of mine. After their first meeting, the man to whom she was promised refused to go through with the marriage. Couldn't Salman simply do something similar?

"I'm really sorry, Salman, but I'd never be a good wife to you. After everything that has happened, I would never be able to love you. Is that what you want? Why don't you tell your father and my mother that you don't want to marry me?"

He stared at me blankly.

"Because I love you. I love you and you will learn to love me too." Saying this, he took the knife and left the kitchen.

Even though Salman walked in, I wouldn't have been capable of hurting myself — and not only because the Islamic faith prohibits suicide. I wouldn't have done it because I wasn't finished with life. I still hoped that I could find a solution. But at the moment I felt utterly helpless.

That same evening, my mother was discharged from the hospital. I was so relieved that she was feeling better and didn't have to stay the night there. The next morning, my mother was able to get up again. Although she didn't say a word about the events of the previous day, I could tell she blamed me for everything. When, on top of everything else, my brother became very sick, my father decided that we would depart earlier than planned. He organized the airline tickets, and we started to say goodbye to the neighbors. I was relieved. My problems wouldn't be getting any smaller, but at least there would once again be six thousand miles separating me from some of them. At least I wouldn't face the disappointed scowls of my relatives everywhere I went. Perhaps everything would turn out all right after all.

In the days before our departure, I tried to be particularly friendly to my aunt and to Salman. I hoped that I could still persuade them to refuse the wedding. But whenever I started to talk about it, he put me off, saying that he would think about it later in peace. I had to be satisfied with that for the time being. Perhaps he would fall in love with somebody else once I had gone back to Austria and reject me for her.

On the day of our departure, I got up early, packed my things, and helped my aunt with the breakfast. She was nice to me, and perhaps she was also a little sad that things had happened the way they did. Shortly after ten o'clock my uncle drove up in a neighbor's car and started to load our luggage together with Salman and my father. All the bags disappeared into the trunk — except for mine.

"You've forgotten my bag," I said.

"No, we haven't." My father's voice was cold.

"What do you mean?"

"We haven't forgotten it. You're not flying with us."

I felt sick. My knees began to shake so badly that I had to sit down on the ground.

"But why? Why am I not flying with you?"

My father stepped up to me and looked me over. It was hot. I saw sweat stains in his armpits and smelled his breath.

"I didn't buy a ticket for you because I didn't want to. I spoke to your grandfather a few days ago. He is of the same opinion as me. We want you to stay here. We want you to live with your aunt and your future husband and become a decent girl. One who behaves and thinks like a proper Pakistani girl," he said, quietly but urgently.

I started to cry. I wanted to say something, but I couldn't.

"How long?" I finally managed to ask.

"Until you are ready to marry Salman."

I was devastated and begged Abba to take me with them, but he refused to change his mind. The only concession he made was to allow me to accompany the family to the airport. In the car, I once again sat in the back seat with my sister Aisha and cried for the entire journey. I couldn't marry Salman, but now I was stuck in Pakistan with no one to help me. My family had abandoned me. I was completely alone.

Abba,

Did you know you were my hero?
I remember when you first left,
Risking everything for a dream,
And journeyed to distant lands.
How many sacrifices did you make,
Stepping into the unknown?

Those years — too many years —
My heart ached with the distance between us,
As I waited, longing for the sight of you,
While you labored far away, earning our bread.
I swallowed my hunger for you,
When I went to bed.

Then, one radiant day,
Your face — sun-kissed and glowing —
Rejoiced with the joy of a thousand suns,
As you saw your little girl.

How simple life felt,
How whole we were in that moment.
In Sarleinsbach, we were one,
Our happiness a fragile, perfect thing.
What could possibly tear it apart?

But only six years —
Six short, fleeting years —
And you were gone again.
Your refusal to love me —
It didn't make sense.
The pain of your rejection,
And emptiness where your love once was.

So many ways I tried to please you —
When Mother hit me, and bruised me,
It was never enough.
I trusted your promises,
Like the little girl you once loved.
But now you, too, left me —
To a man who would abuse me,
Imprison me in his room,
Demanding that I be given to him,
To be his forever,
For the sake of your honor.

And I thought I was still your little girl.
It didn't make sense.
But then I realized,
And I should have known —
That this was my fate from very early on,
To be broken by you for the glory of your tribe,
While I only ever longed for your love.

One day, dear Abba, I wish we will be united again.
When I go to sleep, I carry you in my heart.
It feels a little like death.
And when I awake in the morning, hope resurrects once again.
Maybe one day, after my last Resurrection we will meet again,
In Paradise where the Son of Man dwells. In the Place of Love,
your sun-kissed face will look at me again with gladness.
Then all will make sense,
For then, all will be Love.

6

The Madrassa

Please note that this chapter contains a passage with graphic sexual abuse content.
While this may be disturbing for some readers, the author feels strongly that the episode
is important in understanding her story and it is not presented in a gratuitous manner.
It has been shaded in a grey background for those who wish to skip over the content.

MY PARENTS' DEPARTURE hit me hard. They had left me in a country that I didn't know and where I couldn't find my way around. I felt I was suffocating. There was nobody I could talk to. The only people around were my aunt and Salman, exactly the cause of my problems. I had never in my life felt so lonely and abandoned. Driving back from the airport, I cried ceaselessly. I couldn't and wouldn't calm down.

"Everything will be all right," Salman repeated constantly, sitting with me in the back seat.

"What can possibly turn out all right?" I asked him, even though I knew that he didn't have an answer. I would not fall in love with him. I would not marry him. He was living on another planet if he thought I ever would. Then I realized I was now living on that planet too: Pakistan.

My parents wanted me to develop into a proper Muslim girl, but did they really believe that leaving me here would bring me back to their path? That I would begin a new life? What they thought was adolescent rebellion or the result of too much exposure to Western culture I knew was a matter of survival. I was sixteen years old at the time — I wasn't a child who could be threatened with violence or mental cruelty. I had spent my adolescence in a country where one could find Coca-Cola, cinemas, MTV, and H&M on every street corner; where a girl could meet boys unpunished and spend her afternoons between swimming pools and coffee shops. Not that I had enjoyed all these privileges fully, but I knew that all these things existed, and *that* was my world, not the hell I'd been thrown into. It was too late to groom me into a submissive, obedient wife. I'd developed ideas about the world and where I belonged in it. This wasn't it. When we came back from the airport, my aunt was waiting for us. I was still crying, but my aunt, who in the previous days had made an effort to seem nice, made no move to comfort me.

"Stop whining," she snapped at me. "When I'm finished with your education, you'll know what's right and what's not." I cried the whole night through.

When I woke up the next morning, Salman and my aunt were already dressed. "Get up," my aunt said. "And get dressed. We're going to find a school for you."

The three of us squeezed onto Salman's motorbike and drove off. Initially I thought that if my aunt really was looking for a school for me, perhaps it wouldn't be so bad. Perhaps we might find a school specializing in music or acting. But as we arrived in front of the first school building, I was rudely awakened from my daydream. It was an undistinguished building that was dirty and dusty even on the outside. Suddenly everything became clear: She was going to send me to a Koran school.

In Pakistan, there are normal schools for girls, and then there are Koran schools called *madrassas* — religious seminaries. I had already heard a lot about them, and I was horrified. In many madrassas, hundreds of children are packed together in an airless room where the Koran is read every day from dawn until dusk. The students were not allowed to do anything other than concentrate on the writings of Muhammed. Among the horror stories you hear about these schools is that they are jihad factories, there to produce the next generation of *shaheed* (Muslim martyrs). No one comes to visit them, the hygiene is appalling, and the students are beaten for the slightest mistake. These are the breeding ground for fundamentalist terrorists, and even though I was a believing Muslim at the time, I didn't want to die for Allah anymore.

As we entered the school building, my first glance confirmed all that I had heard. Everything looked exactly the way I imagined it would. I saw dozens of girls in their salwar kameez, most of whom had their hair hidden under a *chador*. Nobody laughed, nobody spoke, and the silence was almost ghostly. Only suras of the Koran were recited.

We went to the school principal and my aunt told him that she wanted to register me at the school. The principal looked at me.

"Where do you come from?" he asked me.

"I was born in Dhadar but I have lived in Austria for the last seven years," I said while looking into his eyes.

He sent me to wait outside the door. Shortly after, my aunt came back out.

"He's refused you," she said. "He doesn't want any European girls at his school." And the fact that I looked at him while speaking to him didn't help. Men and women are not supposed to look at each other.[4]

She was furious, but I heaved a sigh of relief. If none of the madrassas wanted to take a Western girl, I thought, maybe I was in luck. I made sure that the first thing I told each principal was that I'd grown up in Austria. The same thing happened at all the other seminaries. As soon as the principals heard that I came from Austria, they turned me down. One principal even suggested that my aunt send me to a normal school, saying that the conditions would be "almost inhuman" for me. But my aunt pushed on.

---

4   The Koran teaches in sura An-Nur 24:31: "And tell the believing women that they must lower their gazes."

Eventually, she found a madrassa that would take me. She swore that I would not come back until I was the same as the other girls. The school was a Sunni madrassa in the center of Lahore and, even from the outside, it looked menacing: I could see only a long wall of flaking plaster. In the middle were heavy, iron gates that creaked piercingly when they swung open. Behind the gates, grouped around a courtyard, were three flat, single-story buildings that looked as if they were about to collapse. Everywhere the plaster was crumbling from the façades and there were holes in the walls. The inner courtyard was absolutely filthy; stones lay on the ground with half-rotten scraps of food scattered in between — a true paradise for vermin, another level of hell for me. The omnipresent smell of curry was mixed with the scents of decomposing food, feces, and urine.

On entering the courtyard, I had already been struck by how quiet it was. I heard no voices, even though there must have been several hundred girls in the madrassa. The only thing heard was the reciting of the Koran. In Pakistan, it is loud and hectic everywhere, making this silence all the more unsettling.

The principal brought me into a large, dirty, and carpeted room. There was no furniture, just thirty or so girls sitting in rows. I looked around, astonished, and asked the other girls where the dormitory and dining room were. But their giggling told me that neither existed. Of course, there was also no TV, radio, or newspapers. The Islam preached was pure and untainted by the "influence of the infidels." Over the coming months, I was to spend my time almost exclusively in this room. This is where we learned, ate, and slept. Our food was mostly lentils and chickpeas with flatbread or rice. The leftovers were eaten for breakfast. There were no chairs, so we had to kneel on the floor to eat and learn. No air conditioning, and no ventilation either. In the evenings, we lay down on the floor to sleep — there weren't any mattresses, never mind beds.

There were no men to be seen anywhere. And our entire days were devoted to memorizing and reading the Koran in Arabic, a language that none of us understood. But in the Muslim world those who recite and memorize the Koran are considered pious, and those who want to know the meaning are "just" learned. The language is considered important because the Koran was written in Arabic. Muslims often proudly declare that there is no mistake in the Koran because it was perfectly preserved in one tongue.

Madrassas such as this one are common throughout Pakistan and are often funded by the Saudi Arabian royal family. Although they do not arm their students with physical weapons, they give terrorists, such as the Taliban, the ideology and resolve needed to kill in the name of Allah. I still have nightmares about the madrassa. Once I saw a little girl violently brought in screaming, and to this day, when I am feeling weak and hear children scream, it takes me back to that place, where children grow up without a childhood, sitting in small rooms with no windows, no teddies, and no hugs. Some of them sit there for thirteen hours a day. That's what it takes to memorize the Koran as fast as possible.

The worst of the madrassa was the nightmarish bathrooms. For dozens of girls there were only three bathrooms with showers — only one of which worked. We stood in long lines in front of the door waiting our turn. The bathroom itself was tiled, but the tiles were so dirty that I wondered whether they had ever been cleaned. Certainly not this century. There was dirt all over the walls, and when it was hot — as it was practically every day — flies and all kinds of other vermin swarmed the washroom. There were once-white towels with traces of blood on them laying around everywhere. None of my fellow students had ever even heard of a tampon; they used these towels and then simply left them laying in the washroom. There was no other option, and nobody dared complain.

The showers too were beyond description — and not just by Western standards. They were barely large enough to stand in, and although they had doors, the locks didn't work, so you had no privacy whatsoever. The most absurd thing was the shower itself. There wasn't a showerhead as such but at navel height there was a miserable little tap. I had either to kneel down to wash or else use a plastic bucket to awkwardly pour water over my head, which of course took forever. And there was no time, because right outside the next girl was banging on the door, waiting to have her wash. I tried to bathe as fast as I could because, on top of everything else, the water was ice cold.

The toilet was just as unpleasant: It was a hole in the ground, which would have been bearable, except that it regularly flooded and left you standing in feces. Since this was a Pakistani madrassa, it goes without saying that there was no toilet paper, only a bucket with blackish-brown liquid in it with which you were supposed to clean yourself. It was torture, and it took me several days before I could summon the courage to wash myself there. I had no choice.

I immediately felt like a prisoner at the madrassa. My days ran according to a strict schedule with no variation. We were woken shortly before dawn. After *wuzu*, the ceremonial washing, we observed *fadjar*, the morning prayer, then we had our breakfast. There was no school uniform, but we still all looked the same: Most of the girls wore a chador and those who didn't had to tie their hair into a severe knot, as anything else wouldn't have been pleasing to God. "Every hair that a woman shows, will be another snake in her grave when she dies!" I once heard as a child. Otherwise, we were dressed completely in white. White is the color of the Prophet I was told — devout Muslims must not only follow his teachings in their thoughts alone but also in their outward appearance. Those who didn't obey were hit by the supervisor until they did.

The supervisor was one of two people watching over us. She was a tall, gaunt woman. She remained in our room from morning to evening. She oversaw our food distribution, sent us to the washrooms in the mornings, and, during the lesson period when we had to read the Koran, she watched that we did not chat or come up with any other kind of diversion to take our attention away from the Koran. She had the eyes of a hawk and was never without her cane, which she used frequently and with great enthusiasm. If we whispered, laughed, or behaved in some other inappropriate manner, she would hit us with the cane five times, at least.

Apart from the readings, which took place in the morning, afternoon, and evening, a mullah came by each morning to give us lessons. For two hours every day, we read the Koran and he explained the words of the Prophet.

"*Lakdio Parda Karo!*" the supervisor cried whenever the mullah appeared, which meant: "Girls, cover yourselves, the mullah is coming." And we would hide our faces behind our veils and go into the classroom. The mullah was not allowed to see women, so the room was split by a curtain during this class. He sat behind the curtain, while we sat on the other side in two rows of fifteen. In front of us there was a table fifteen feet long and twenty inches high on which the Koran was placed. It was the only piece of furniture in the room. Unlike us, the Koran is never allowed to lie on the ground. And we sat before it cross-legged, moving back and forth with our upper bodies. Otherwise it was impossible to sit all day like this.

"*Asalam alaikum wa rehmatullah*. Peace be with you." Those were his first words every day. He would then decide which sura of the Koran would be read that day and begin the lesson. There was absolute silence as he taught, because nobody was allowed to ask questions.

The mullah knew that there was a European girl in the class, but he did not want to ask me himself why I was there. One day he heard me crying in class.

"Who's that crying?" the mullah asked.

"The girl from Austria," the other girls answered.

He asked me to come to him. I stood up, tugged my salwar kameez properly into place, and went to the front.

"No, don't pull back the curtain. It's forbidden!" the others shouted as they saw me reaching out my hand to push the curtain aside. I was confused. Did he want to speak to me or not?

"What's your name and why are you crying, girl?" the mullah asked.

"My name is Sabatina. And I can't stand it here anymore," I sniffed.

"Allah has chosen you, Sabatina. That is why you are allowed to attend a madrassa. That is a gift, a stroke of luck, and that's why you should be pious and not cry."

But this thought couldn't comfort me either. The promise of Paradise was not enough to make me forget the fact that my own parents had abandoned me.

Lessons and readings went on until the evening. They were interrupted only by prayers: The *fajr* prayer is usually around 4:15 in the morning, the *zohar* prayer sometime between noon and one, the *assar* prayer at four in the afternoon, the *maghrib* prayer at seven in the evening, and the *isha* prayer at nine o'clock. We had to perform our ritual ablutions before each prayer. There was only one break during the whole day, one hour after noon, when we were allowed to move around in the classroom or in the courtyard. This was also when we ate. The day ended after the *isha* prayer around midnight.

In addition to reading the Koran, the teachers drilled into us all the rules and proscriptions that a Pakistani woman had to observe. That a woman may never wear her hair loose, because this is unchaste. That one should not drink while standing, because this is how the Prophet Muhammed drank. That a woman is unclean when menstruating and may therefore not touch the Koran during this period; someone else has to open it for her.

My fellow students either weren't bothered by the monotony and rules, or they had already been broken by them. Most of them were about my age, and everyone shared the same expressionless, apathetic face. There was nothing to get excited about, no reason to laugh. There wasn't even any reason to cry. These girls had been cut off from the outside world and lived in their rut of praying, reading the Koran, and sleeping.

The days wore by unbearably slowly. I thought about my family almost the entire time. Why had they done this to me? Because I didn't want to marry Salman? I was depressed and longed for Linz and my old life. And despite the fact that I was confused and hurt by my parents' abandonment, I missed my family desperately. My father had promised to pick me up "sometime," and I believed in this vague promise and held on to it tightly. Only — when? I can still remember the countless times I begged Allah to deliver me and send my father to get me. But nothing happened.

I never settled in. As time went on, I became more and more certain that I wouldn't survive this torment, even though I couldn't say exactly what the worst torment was: the disgusting and unsanitary conditions, the strict supervisors, the boredom of being locked inside every day and vegetating in this rut, or being left behind by my parents.

Although I lived with the other girls in such a small space, I had hardly any contact with them. They couldn't understand why I found it so difficult and had little sympathy for my problems with my family and my refusal to marry my cousin.

"What is so bad if your parents chose a husband for you?" they asked me. For them, this prospect was completely normal. Most of them were already promised to somebody. Many would never see their husbands before they married. Love and affection were foreign concepts to them, something that Allah might bestow as an extra gift in Paradise. In the West — and particularly in America where people take their freedom for granted — some more traditionally minded women romanticize the idea of an "arranged marriage." But what I saw there in the madrassa was its harsh reality: Arranged marriage means the loss of freedom, the loss of free will. To be forced into lifelong union with a man you don't love, let alone like, is a forced marriage — a lifetime of rape.

Most of the time, talking was prohibited during the day. If a girl spoke too loudly, the supervisor would hit her without warning. Sometimes we had to assemble in the courtyard, where the teachers would make an example of one of the students. Again and again, one of the girls would be caned in front of all of us for some trifle, with the result being that the poor girl would hardly be able to sit down because of pain. Luckily, I kept my head down and never had to submit to such punishments, but watching was unpleasant enough.

During the breaks I usually sat alone in a corner of the courtyard and looked sadly at the pictures of my friends in Austria. "What will they think?" I asked myself. I had promised to write to them from Pakistan but that hadn't been possible. Once, I tried to write a letter to my girlfriends, but the letter was taken away from me. And that was that.

Slowly the madrassa began to break me. I became increasingly lethargic and cheerless and dragged myself heavily from one dismal school day to the next.

I made only one friend at the Koran school. Her name was Zahra, and she was the same age as I was and came from a little village more than sixty miles north of Lahore. She had had a difficult childhood, as her parents had died when she was still small. When she was five years old, she was taken in by her aunt, who hit her constantly. She was also repeatedly abused by her uncle, which her aunt never tried to stop. For Zahra, the madrassa was paradise because she finally had escaped the abuse.

She was the only one who made an effort to understand me. Although she had also been brought up on the teachings of the Koran and had never left Pakistan, she wasn't quite as narrow-minded as the other girls. She asked me lots of questions about Austria and life outside Pakistan, although it was obviously difficult for her to take in everything I told her about life there.

Zahra was an anchor for me during this period and comforted me when I was overwhelmed at night by homesickness or when I woke up in the middle of the night crying. She also stood up for me when I was teased by the other girls and didn't leave my side when I told her I didn't know how I was going to survive the next meal. From the beginning, I could scarcely eat the food that they served us every day.

The evening meal in particular, which usually consisted of *dal,* an indefinable soup made of red lentils, and *roti,* a flatbread, was the worst.

Before the meal, I would go with Zahra to wash my hands. There was always a long line for the washbasin, so we had to wait a while for our turn. When it was finally my turn, my eye settled first on the pile of bloodstained towels laying amid all the filth and vermin at the edge of the washbasin. I would feel a wave of nausea rising in me and would rush, closely followed by Zahra, to the toilet.

I simply couldn't eat after having to use those toilets, which were constantly flooded and stank of urine, excrement, and vomit. I had been continuously nauseous since my arrival at the Koran school two months before — until one day I finally refused to eat. My memories of this dismal period are patchy and blurred. The endless monotony not only drove me to my physical limit but systematically worked its way into my mind, gradually wearing down my resistance. It was subtle brainwashing, although not in the way that my parents, my aunt, and the Koran school teachers had imagined. I hadn't become a proper Pakistani girl who was looking forward to her wedding and raising her husband's family, as they hoped. Instead, I was sad and apathetic; I wasn't even interested in learning, which I had once enjoyed so much.

It took the supervisors several weeks to notice that I had become increasingly hollow-cheeked and lethargic. When I then caught lice on top of everything else and lay sick with severe diarrhea, they finally contacted my aunt. My torment was finally over, but when my aunt came to get me, I was so despondent and weak that I barely even noticed.

When I returned to my aunt and uncle's house, I had changed. The three months I had spent in this madrassa had done their job.

It wasn't that I had changed my mind about marrying Salman, but the attempts of the supervisor and the mullah to discipline me had clearly borne fruit. I also came to realize that Islam was on my parents' side and the Prophet Muhammed, whom I had always imagined as a loving man, was in fact the one who allowed all this to happen to me. I was broken. When my aunt spoke to me, I didn't try to converse with her but simply listened without comment. My resistance to my aunt and my parents, which had been the most important thing to me just months before, had disappeared. I didn't see the sense any longer in rebelling against everything and everybody. I didn't want to be beaten and shouted at anymore. So I gave up.

I was extremely thin. My cheeks had fallen in and there were dark rings under my eyes. But thanks to my aunt's generous cooking my condition improved and, only a week later, I had more or less recovered. But if I believed that the madrassa chapter of my life was now over, I was soon to find out how wrong I was. I had hardly recovered physically when my aunt went off in search of a new madrassa. My aunt was certain that despite my newly submissive demeanor, my religious education was far from complete.

We found a Wahhabi madrassa in the immediate vicinity of our house. Here too the focus was on learning the teachings of Muhammed. The twenty-five girls in my class were just as devout but far friendlier and more open-minded than my previous classmates, which was surprising, since the Wahhabis are one of the strictest Islamic schools. Unlike at the other school, we were allowed to talk and stand around together in the courtyard during breaks. "Allah gave you a beautiful face!" one of the girls would exclaim. "And your cousin isn't even twice your age — you're lucky." Sometimes, we even laughed together while kneeling on the carpets before the low wooden bench where the Koran rested. The supervisor had a lot of children. She was married to an old man at just thirteen and was deeply conservative. She often urged us to wear gloves and cover one of our eyes, believing it would help conceal the "evil" within women's bodies and protect us from rape.

This madrassa was not a boarding school. My cousin Salman brought me there every day before he went to school and then picked me up every evening. And finally, I had something approximating a family with whom I could talk, even if it was only my aunt and cousins. I was still not allowed to leave the house alone. This upset me considerably. Nevertheless, I made no attempt to rebel. Because he could go off on his own, Salman was responsible for the household shopping. When he drove off every few days on his motorbike and came back laden with groceries and other supplies, I burned with envy. I had been in Pakistan for more than four months, most of which I'd spent in the madrassa or my aunt's house.

On my seventeenth birthday, as a surprise, Salman said he would take me on a drive — so long as I remained fully covered. He drove me to Defence, a district I had heard a great deal about since my arrival in Pakistan. It was said that the rich and the beautiful of Lahore — the politicians, musicians, and professional athletes — lived here. It was said to be almost like the West.

On our way over, I noticed that the roads were becoming broader and better, and the area was quieter and cleaner. There were no garbage bags laying around in the street and it didn't stink as terribly as the other neighborhoods we'd driven through. Modern, Western-looking houses stood next to fancy restaurants and bars. I recognized the names of numerous international companies, and the people I saw wore Western clothing. Salman parked the motorbike in a small square and we got off. I wanted to go to the local McDonald's, but he refused. And when I asked if we could just walk around instead, he shut that down too. "A friend of mine might see us," he said. "It would be disgraceful for me because we're not married yet."

I had only wanted to see something other than the madrassa. And now here I was — only to once again be looking at life from the outside. I cried and we went home. That was the extent of my birthday excursion.

Soon I came to terms with my situation. When my cousins were at school, I stayed alone with my aunt, who didn't talk to me, but who at least didn't scold me anymore. Very occasionally, I was lucky enough to have the house to myself. On those days I climbed up onto the flat roof and listened to music on my Walkman. Those were my most beautiful moments in Pakistan. I can still remember them clearly — the peacefulness of the neighborhood, the pleasure of listening to music that made me happy — but then again, I had very few beautiful moments in Pakistan.

One day, I was sitting on the roof when my aunt rushed into the house. She could hardly breathe. After she had collected herself, she told me that a girl in a nearby neighborhood had hanged herself because she was raped. The offender lived two streets away. My aunt knew him.

"Have the police arrested him yet?" I asked.

"No, how could they?" she replied. "He is a man, and the girl tempted him. It was her own fault."

I was filled with horror. When my aunt told me about the girl's rape and suicide, I understood more clearly than I had during my stay at the madrassa. A woman in Pakistan has no value whatsoever. I knew that I could never survive here. I had to get out as soon as possible.

I knew my relationship with my parents was troubled, but I still loved them. Suddenly, in comparison to the madness and suffocation of my life in Pakistan, the beatings and endless humiliations I had experienced at my parents' hands seemed relatively minor. Despite the abuse, I missed my parents and wanted to go home. I wanted to go back without having the faintest notion of how this might be accomplished. I spoke to my aunt a few times, but she only gave me evasive replies.

Salman knew that he was the most important person in the household and that he could have anything he wanted. He exploited this power over his mother and sisters — and me. He was in love with me; that was clear enough. He was certain that we would be married one day, whether I liked it or not, and I clearly didn't. This obviously fed his fantasies, as I could increasingly tell from his looks. Whenever he felt himself unobserved, I could feel him staring at me and see the expectant glow in his eyes.

Since my birthday, he tried repeatedly to be alone with me, practically every evening in fact. I, on the other hand, made every effort to avoid such situations. I didn't want anything from him, and I knew being alone with him was a bad idea. I also didn't want to drag my aunt into the whole business because I could guess what she would say. In Pakistan, young people are not allowed to have any sort of physical contact before marriage. Even kissing is forbidden. If anyone found out that something had happened between Salman and me, the entire family would have been disgraced. And after seeing her reaction to our neighbor's rape and suicide, it didn't take much imagination to figure out who my aunt would blame.

I told Salman to leave me alone, but he didn't listen. For this reason, I tried to stay out of his way wherever possible. But one night, about two weeks after my birthday, everything changed.

It was long after midnight and I had already been sleeping for some time when I suddenly felt something touching me. I sat up and looked around me. To my left lay my cousins Habiba and Bahar, both fast asleep. I turned around. It was Salman, who had snuck in. I could hear quiet, monotonous snoring from the corner where my aunt slept. I looked up at Salman, who placed his forefinger to his lips and signaled to me that I should follow him outside.

I was in a predicament. On the one hand I didn't want to go outside with him because I could easily guess what would happen. On the other hand, I didn't want to raise the alarm because I couldn't figure out what the consequences might be. But he refused to leave, so in the end I gave up and went with him. He pulled me into his room. Apart from the muffled noise of the street coming through the window, it was completely quiet.

We stood beside his bed. He stretched out his hand and touched my hair. Then he stroked my cheek and slowly ran his forefinger across my lips. I felt dirty, disgusting, nauseated. Salman drew me toward him, closed his eyes, and bent forward to kiss me. Then he started to push away my clothes and kiss my breast. I felt sick. I wanted to run away but my legs were paralyzed. Then he pulled down his trousers and started to masturbate. It was the most humiliating experience I could imagine. I was so disgusted that I wanted to vomit, but I couldn't. Instead, I stayed completely still and looked at him — looked at him staring at my breasts. I despised him. I waited until he was finished before I turned away and returned to my bed without deigning to give him another look. I couldn't even cry.

The next day I didn't speak a single word to Salman, but that didn't seem to bother him. He acted as if nothing had happened. From then on, it happened almost every night. As soon as the others were asleep, Salman crept into our room and fetched me. I tried to show him that it left me cold, so that after a few attempts he at least didn't make any effort to kiss me beforehand. Instead, I looked on blankly. Then I wiped his semen off my body and left the room without looking at him again.

But inside I was boiling. The bulimia from which I had suffered since the beginning of my mother's abuse only got worse. A few times my aunt heard me vomiting in the toilet. She said that I was possessed by a demon. I was so disgusted that I couldn't even look at myself in the mirror. I hated being a woman, hated being in Pakistan, hated having to be inside this body.

By this time, I had been in Pakistan for more than five months. I rarely heard from my parents because when they called, they spoke almost exclusively with my aunt. I was still thinking constantly about home and wanted to go back as soon as possible, but I no longer cried about it. Unexpectedly, I had resigned myself to my lot.

Living in Pakistan hadn't damaged my faith in Allah. As before, I was still a devout Muslim and prayed five times a day. Unlike the other girls in my class, I often asked questions when I didn't understand something. All girls and boys in madrassa learn the Koran in Arabic and no one understands what they are reading. But I wanted to know. Had the Prophet really said that? Did Allah really will that the world be this way? I hoped that perhaps in Paradise we women would be honored.

I was still proud to be a Muslim and felt my religion was far superior to others. But that was only the religious aspect: I still didn't want to be a Pakistani housewife. There must be a way to live with a Western value system and be a devout Muslim, I thought.

My aunt recognized my obvious transformation and alerted other members of my family that I was becoming docile. Unexpectedly, my grandfather arrived from Dhadar. I knew that he was there to monitor my development. I behaved as submissively as I could — didn't ask a single question, recited the verses of the Koran that I had learned by heart, and only spoke when spoken to. When he left the following day, I had the feeling that I had passed the test.

When my aunt was present, I tried to be particularly friendly to my cousin Salman. I chatted with him and brought him water or chai without being asked. I didn't let on in any way that he was still violating me almost every night. And, as I had foreseen, my aunt took a positive view of this change in my attitude to Salman.

"Are you ready to marry him now?" she asked me one day.

"Yes," I answered and looked down at the ground, just like a proper Pakistani girl.

A few days before Christmas, my mother called my aunt again. She spoke for some time before my aunt finally passed me the receiver.

"I hear that you have changed," my mother said. She sounded uncharacteristically nice.

"Yes," I replied.

"An angel will be coming for you in a few days," she continued.

I didn't quite understand what she was talking about — and I didn't want to get my hopes up. For the next few days, I was so excited that I could hardly sleep at night, but I couldn't take the slightest chance of blowing my cover by letting anything slip. Secretly, of course, I hoped that my parents were coming to get me, although I forbade myself to dwell on this thought. What if they were only visiting and then went back without me? I couldn't go through that again.

One day, shortly after noon, I heard the car in the driveway. I ran out of the room, tore the gate open, and threw myself into his arms.

Abba. I never wanted to let go. He had come for me, and he wouldn't leave me alone here again.

"I'm so happy to see you," I said.

"So am I." He took a step back and looked at me.

"I see *nur* in your face," he said, and laughed.

Nur is the Pakistani expression for calmness and inner balance, the quality they'd hoped to develop in me when they left me.

We went into the house and my aunt told my father how much I had changed. That I prayed, that I was happy going to the madrassa, and that I helped her in the house. My father seemed very proud of me, and happy. I was even happier. Now everything would be all right, I thought.

"Are you ready to marry Salman now?" he asked me with a serious expression.

"If you wish it, I am," I answered.

He hugged me, and my aunt's face lit up in a broad smile.

After that, everything had to go very quickly, as my father had so little time. His return flight was booked for the first of January — and this time he had bought a ticket for me as well.

There wasn't enough time and money for a proper wedding, because our relatives from Dhadar and my mother and siblings in Austria couldn't get there so quickly, so my father and aunt decided that Salman and I should just become engaged for the time being. After that, I would travel with my father to Austria and complete my education. We would marry in the next few years. I was happier than I'd ever been. Not because I was marrying Salman, but because my torment was finally coming to an end.

Over the next few days a handful of relatives arrived: one of my aunts, an uncle, and, of course, my grandfather the imam, who would perform the religious ceremony.

December 31 was the day. That morning my aunt and cousins helped me to dress. I wore a red salwar kameez that my aunt had chosen especially for the occasion and black shoes. At the house we found that neighbors had arrived alongside our relatives. All the women from the neighborhood had cooked so much that the tables were filled with Pakistani delicacies: huge pots of basmati rice and untold quantities of chicken in curry sauce that were cooked only for feast days. *Paratha,* a particularly delicious type of flatbread baked only for special occasions, was laid out on another table. For dessert there was sweet rice and *mithai,* a Pakistani candy.

All my cousins gathered around me and excitedly asked me how I was feeling.

"Great. I'm so happy," I said politely.

Shortly after midday I was called into the living room. Just like six months before when I had refused to marry Salman, the family council was once again sitting on the sofa: my father, several uncles, my mother's father, and, of course, my grandfather in the middle. When I entered the room, they all stood up. Salman was nowhere to be seen.

My grandfather started to recite some verses of the Koran, of which I didn't understand a single word. The whole thing lasted only a few minutes and then I was told to leave the room again. I had signed nothing, done nothing. That's it? I thought.

After me, Salman was then called into the room, where he underwent the same procedure.

The whole affair wasn't particularly exciting. Of course, it was only an engagement and not a wedding, where there would have been music and festivities lasting two days, with the bride brought by car to the bridegroom.

The neighbors and relatives started eating and spent the rest of the afternoon together chatting, while I spent most of the time with my cousins and the neighbors' children in the living room. Now and again Salman looked in, dressed festively and beaming. I couldn't fail to notice that he kept trying to be alone with me, while I made every effort to stay away from him. When it was finally time to sleep, my little cousins came to my rescue — unwittingly. "We're sleeping with Sabatina tonight, because she's leaving tomorrow," they called, and I seized the opportunity and hurried with them to the women's room. The next morning, we actually left. More than six months after he'd left me in Pakistan, my father brought me back to Austria.

Before our departure at the airport, my cousin said to me, forcing the words out: "You were only pretending, weren't you, Sabatina?" I turned around and disappeared through passport control without a reply. Finally, I thought, my nightmare was over.

7

Joseph's Gift

THE ENGAGEMENT HAD gained me time and gotten me a ticket out of Pakistan, but the ordeal wasn't over yet. At some point my family would insist that our betrothal be followed up by a wedding. We landed in Vienna January 2, 2000, around midday. Even though we'd had layovers in Dubai and London, I wasn't tired at all. Pakistan was behind me. I was home.

I saw my mother again for the first time in the arrivals hall at the Vienna airport. She had come with an Indian friend and her husband from Linz to collect us, as she had no driver's license. Although I hadn't forgotten what had happened between us over the previous two years, I was still happy and relieved to finally see her again. We fell into each other's arms.

In Linz nothing appeared to have changed — our house, the used car dealer beside us, Sylvia's hair salon on the corner. In the photo shop on the ground floor of our building, the same portraits were hanging in the window as when I had left, and our neighbor's silver VW Passat was still parked in its usual place, right beside the old red Mercedes, which was only slightly younger than its owner. I felt like I had been away half a lifetime, but in fact barely six months had passed.

My brothers behaved as usual: very casual, as if they couldn't care less that I was back. But I could see that they were happy. And then I saw my sister, who was like a different person. When we parted at the airport in Lahore, she had cried bitter tears and clung on to me so tight that my mother had to drag her away from me, but now she simply stood at the door and displayed no emotion.

"Hello," was all she said before disappearing into our room.

We went into the kitchen, and I had my first opportunity to talk in detail about my time in Pakistan. Unlike my father, my mother wanted to know every single detail and listened intently as I told her about the madrassas, my cousins, my aunt, and Salman. And she dug deeper when she had the feeling that I was leaving something out — which I was. I avoided telling her about the way I had been degraded by Salman because I didn't want her to blame me, or suspect that I was pretending to have reformed in order to escape the situation. Apparently, my narrative was convincing enough.

"You have *nur* in your face," she said, smiling, when I had finished talking.

This was exactly what my father had said to me in Lahore. She concluded that it had been a good idea for me to spend six months in Pakistan, "being educated," as she put it.

I didn't leave the apartment for the first few days.

Above all, I continued to pray regularly. This was one clear effect of the madrassa: Although I had practiced before, I had now become an even more devout Muslim. Islam was the only true religion, and I was proud to be Muslim. I recited all five prayers required of a practicing Muslim, and I read several suras every day, just as I had learned to do in Pakistan. The more you read the Koran (even without understanding it), the more *sawaab* (merit) you get. Prophet Muhammed said: "Whoever recites a letter from the Book of Allah, he will receive one good deed as ten good deeds like it."

This provided me with an anchor. It distracted me and gave me one constant in my life, even if everything around me was out of control. For the time being, that was enough.

Soon after we arrived, my father grabbed some sweets as a gift and took me to Farah's house. My father hoped he could regain his honor within the Muslim community and Farah's family. I was so excited to see her again after so much time had passed. My heart beat wildly. Dad rang the doorbell and her father, Asif, answered.

"*Salam al Eikum* (Peace be upon you), brother. We bring candy as a bearer of a beautiful message: My daughter and Salman are engaged."

But Asif was not pleased with our visit.

"We don't want to have anything to do with the engagement of your daughter! *Khuda Hafiz*! Goodbye!" he replied and slammed the door. Dad and I stood there stunned, with the sweets in our hands. I hoped that Farah would defend me, but she didn't even show her face. "My poor Father, I thought. They will always treat him as an outcast — just because I wanted to be free."

A week later, the school holidays were over for my sister and brothers, and I too wanted to return to my old school, so my father rang the principal on the first day and asked him if I could go back to my old class. But it wasn't that easy. After all, it was already after Christmas and the greater part of the school year was already over. The principal suggested that I should repeat the sixth year of the baccalaureate school, but since I had already lost two years since our move to Austria, losing yet another year and going to class with people younger was out of the question.

"Then go to work," my mother suggested.

But I couldn't accept that. What would guarantee that I wouldn't be sent back to Pakistan to marry Salman if I wasn't going to school?

"Father, you promised me in Pakistan that I could go back to school. I have done everything you wanted. I've even become engaged to Salman. Please let me finish school."

He agreed and started to look for a school for me. A week later I started evening classes in the center of Linz. Classes were held every evening from about six until ten, which naturally didn't please my parents, as it meant that I wouldn't get home until late. But when I reminded my father that he had always wanted me to have a proper education, he finally agreed.

Although I was a little out of practice from being in Pakistan, I coped well with the lessons, the teachers were nice, and I got on well with my fellow students, most of whom were considerably older than I was and already working. Mostly, I was happy to be back in Linz at last.

To avoid fresh trouble with my parents, I hadn't sought out any contact with my old schoolmates, but in such a small city it was only a question of time. Soon enough, I ran into Joseph, a boy who used to be in my other baccalaureate school. The last time I had seen him, nine months before, Joseph had been a skater who wore white T-shirts, sneakers, a baseball cap, and a pair of pants with the crotch hanging down to the knee. He used to hang out with a guy with dreadlocks in the smokers' corner of the school. Now Joseph would read verses from the Bible to me in every break. He brought the Bible to school.

"I have found Jesus," he said. "I've become a Christian."

Joseph's father was a non-practicing Algerian Muslim and his mother a Catholic from Eastern Europe. Given such wildly different backgrounds, Joseph made a choice similar to many people and became an Evangelical Christian.

One day we skipped English class and met up in a coffee shop. He sat in the farthest corner, and I was once again struck by how different he was from all the other students: serious, well-behaved, and so kind. Although we hadn't seen each other for so long, we chatted with ease. We talked about old times and the people we had been to school with, until he finally asked me for the "long story" about my time in Pakistan. But since I wasn't ready to tell him everything about my six months in Pakistan, I quickly changed the subject and asked what had happened to him. He told me everything he learned from the Bible, "his relationship" with his God, and the pastors who lived in his building. They had transformed his life.

I'd been studying the Koran a lot longer than Joseph had been reading the Bible. I felt that I was pretty well-versed in questions of religion, and even if Christianity had been shrugged off at the madrassa as the confusion of Western minds, his story still seemed far-fetched to me. Why should God — whether Allah, the Christian God, or the Jewish God — want a relationship with a creature? I had learned that one should fear Allah in order to be rewarded with Paradise after death. I had been taught by the imam that the only purpose of life is to follow the rules that Muhammed himself practiced in order to go to Heaven. My faith did not allow for a relationship with God or spiritual revelations that influenced one's earthly actions.

Joseph was interesting because like me he took his faith seriously. Whenever I told him about a problem, he immediately started praying, not caring what other people might think when they passed by as we sat in a shopping mall close to the school. He lived as if there were only him and his God in this world.

These days, when I think of him, the verse of St. Augustine comes to my mind: "Love and then do whatever you will." I wanted someone who loved me just the way I was. Joseph was a good listener and funny at the same time. We started to meet almost every day. We sat in front of the school in a coffee shop, met during school breaks, and sometimes even went strolling along the Danube River after school — but only if the last class was canceled, because I had promised my parents to be back home half an hour after school was over at the latest, and I was keeping that promise.

I also started working as a waitress in a coffee shop that offered the local Austrian pastries. Since school didn't start until the evening, my parents thought it would be a good idea for me to earn some money — though it wasn't really *my* money. For instance, with my first paycheck I bought a gray suit for my father. It filled me with joy to have done something that made him happy. The rest of my paychecks were usually sent back to Pakistan. Just as my father worked to support the family back home, so did I. It never bothered me: We were more fortunate than they were. I am still happy that my money paid for my grandfather's eye surgery, without which he would have gone blind.

Although I liked to work in the coffee shop, I mostly looked forward to seeing Joseph. He was just different. While everyone else was uncomfortable talking about religious matters, he read the Bible to me during every break. I found this astonishing because, like many Muslims, I believed that Christians didn't talk much about their faith because deep down they knew that its tenets — here I was thinking of the Trinity in particular — were corrupt. Meanwhile, we Muslims treasured conversation about God and we saw it as our duty to bring Islam to Christians, who mean well but don't know God. Otherwise, wouldn't they speak to us about him?

And so I was puzzled by Joseph. What made him so confident about Christianity? In addition to his kind self-assurance, he was also obliging and helpful, making him completely different from Pakistani men — especially my fiancé, Salman. I enjoyed my walks with Joseph as much as when we were simply sitting on the banks of the Danube or on the main square in Linz without talking. At those moments I would inhale deeply, look at all the people, and listen to the screeching of the tram as it stopped. All of this was freedom for me, and so utterly different from Pakistan where, only a few weeks before, I had been imprisoned in a madrassa.

Joseph and I would talk about anything and everything except my time in Pakistan. He had no idea what I had been through, and I didn't want to tell him. Still, he was my only friend and my best friend. My engagement to Salman was my greatest problem, and I was afraid of how Joseph would react. Deep down, I think I already knew that he would suggest a solution that was too dangerous for me at that point — a solution I didn't even dare to think about. The cost for Muslims to accept Christianity is a tremendous one. I would be ostracized in my community, and all my lifelong relationships that I had built from childhood would be gone. I would be rejected by my friends and relatives, and I didn't want to think of how my parents would react. Acknowledging the God of Christians would mean destroying myself and my family.

Besides, I worried that Joseph would cut off contact with me if I told him too much. All my other old friends had. For them, someone with my level of problems was just *too much*.

All the same, the more time I spent with Joseph, the more deeply I thought about him. He was considerate and helpful, full of joy. The first thing I would see was his smile. He had the courage to express his faith in front of everyone. I could not fathom how he, as a practicing Christian, treated me better than any Muslim did. Was it really his faith that had brought all this about?

As a result, I started to become more interested in Christianity. How was it possible that human creatures could have a personal relationship with God? It was something I'd never considered before, and that question engaged me more than any other. Were these the first seeds of a conflict of faith? Surely not. I was still firmly convinced that Islam was the only true religion. But I had begun to be fascinated by Christianity — especially as my problems at home started to worsen again.

As his fiancée, my parents wanted me to organize a visa for Salman so that he could visit me and stay in Austria. The idea of sharing my life in Linz with Salman terrified me. I vehemently rejected the suggestion, but my parents didn't give up. Again and again, they would tell me that Salman had called and asked for me, that he had a right to see me. It was my duty to apply for a visa for him. I hoped that they would simply give up after a while. I played for time and constantly thought up fresh excuses for why I couldn't.

But they became suspicious and began to monitor my every step, shouting at me if I was even a minute late coming home. I had been careful not to let anything slip about Joseph, fearing that they would forbid me to have contact with him.

The situation was worsening all the time — especially after Pakistanis who sold newspapers in the streets saw me with Joseph and started speaking badly about me within the community. As she had a year before, my mother spied on me getting off the tram from the kitchen window. And it always came back to Salman. Although they didn't threaten to hit me, they made it unmistakably clear that I must arrange for Salman to come to Austria.

"You're just like you were before," my mother said when I resisted. "If you don't bring him over soon, we'll invite him ourselves — but then you're no longer our daughter!"

I'd always known that this moment would come one day, but I had assumed that they would at least let me finish school before the business with Salman got really serious. They kept putting pressure on me, but when I asked them why everything had to move so fast, they had no answer.

Like in Pakistan, I turned to the Koran. The many prayers and reading didn't help. Nothing changed, absolutely nothing.

One day I finally poured my heart out to Joseph during one of our walks. I left nothing out: my problems with my parents, our trip to Pakistan, the madrassa, my forced engagement to Salman, and my parents' constant demand that I arrange a visa for him.

"You must pray and then God will help you," Joseph said when I had finished.

"I pray five times a day, but nothing happens," I replied.

"Have you ever thought that maybe you're praying to the wrong god?" he said.

Looking back now, I realize that Joseph couldn't have said anything else. He was genuinely in love with his God, and it overflowed to me.

His question was also a blasphemy. In Pakistan he would be serving a life sentence or would be given the death penalty under section 295-A of the Penal Code.

And although I believed that my faith was absolutely firm and contradicted him vehemently, his question had an effect on me. I couldn't avoid admitting that Joseph's God played an enormous role in his life, whereas I had yet to see any evidence of mine. Although I resisted these burgeoning thoughts with all my strength, because I didn't want to be faced with what I could have to pay, I did indeed begin to ask myself whether Allah really was the right god. If he was my God, why wasn't he helping me? If I was doing everything I was supposed to do — obeying my parents, praying the *namaz*, reading the Koran — why did everything keep getting worse? Why did I feel like I was being punished?

I was already terrified of the "tortures of the grave," which could only be escaped by dying as a martyr. And I had been convinced that each and every unconcealed hair on a woman's head would mean another snake at her grave. This image unnerved me and filled me with so much fear that I was troubled with nightmares night after night. After all, I wore no headscarf in Austria, and now Joseph had placed a seed of doubt about Allah's existence in me. I was convinced that yet another curse would befall me.

For months I tormented myself with my doubts. The more my parents urged me to bring Salman to Austria, the more unbearable my inner conflict became. I didn't want him to come to Austria and at the same time I didn't want to fuel fresh conflict with my parents. I simply wanted to live my life in peace, finish school, and find a good job, but my parents would never accept this. In order to live in peace, I would have to leave them — something I could scarcely imagine doing. Desperately I looked for the help which my faith and my Muslim community couldn't give me. I looked for answers in the Koran and failed to find them. Everything hinged on the fearful attitude with which infidels should be treated and what one must practice on earth to be rewarded in Heaven. But at that moment I couldn't think about Heaven. After all, my problem — the impossibility of ever marrying Salman — wasn't taking place in the afterlife but right here and now in the present.

There was nobody with whom I could talk, in whom I could confide. My brothers? Completely out of the question. My little sister? She, who had once comforted me, was now so indifferent that she certainly wouldn't have understood. And Joseph? I couldn't talk to him because his faith would make me question my own even more. I was going around in circles and didn't know what to do.

Shortly before Christmas, Joseph invited me to a coffee house in Linz.

"I have a present for you! It's the most valuable thing I can give you," he announced. I was curious to open the beautifully packed gift. It was a Bible! Even though I knew that the possession of this book was an incalculable risk for me, I accepted it.

Meanwhile, the pressure being put on me by my parents ballooned even more. They wanted me to sign the marriage certificate so that they could request the visa for Salman. One night, in desperation I called out to God: "Who are you? Are you Allah, Jesus, Buddha, Krishna? Why, if you are all-powerful and all-knowing, do you not help me now?"

My gaze fell on the Bible.

"This book is a complete falsehood!" my dad had always said. He once even tried to convince a door-to-door Christian missionary of this. And now I, his daughter, held the book of the infidels in my hands. Of course, I had no notion of who the Apostle Paul was or the difference between the New Testament and the Old Testament. Most Muslims don't. I know of an Indian Muslim woman who used to say that Christians wrote the New Testament because the strictures of the Old Testament were too difficult — so that they could dress in bikinis and not feel guilty. Strange as that may sound, this kind of speculation about Christianity is not uncommon at a Muslim dinner table.

But in my case, I was driven to the book of the Christians in search of the answer to just one question: "God, who are you?" I opened the Bible at random and read the following words: "You will seek me and find me when you seek me with all your heart" (Jer. 29:13). Although it wasn't as though I'd been struck by lightning, it felt like this passage was answering my question. I closed it immediately. I never experienced such a thing with the Koran. In Islam, it is forbidden to question the Koran, but this God had told me to seek Him out.

I began to read more. Now that I had a comparison, the harshness of Muhammed's teachings became increasingly obvious to me, especially when I read the Scripture about Mary Magdalene and how Jesus saved her from her accusers. I saw myself in Mary Magdalene, who faced a mob eager to execute her. It was like the mob in Pakistan that surrounded the victim and accused her. Here He comes, the God of the Christians who saves her. Jesus was beautiful. In Islam she would have been executed.

I began making mental comparisons between Muhammed and Jesus and found that the former was the opposite of the latter. When an adulterous woman was brought to Muhammed: stoning for the woman (Sahih Muslim 1:33). But when the same was brought to Jesus: mercy (John 8:7). Muhammed said: "Kill the infidels wherever you find them" (Koran, sura 9:5). Jesus said: "Love your enemies and pray for those who persecute you" (Matt. 5:44). Muhammed said: "I have been commanded to fight against people till they testify that there is no God but Allah, and that Muhammed is the messenger of Allah" (Sahih Muslim 22). Jesus said: "Blessed are the peacemakers" (Matt. 5:9). Muhammed participated in more than twenty-seven battles and wiped out entire tribes of Jews to establish his religion. Jesus said to His executioner, "My kingdom is not of this world" (John 18:36). On and on the list went in my head — no two men could be more different.

But most of all, I was struck by this difference: Allah has ninety-nine names, but the Christian God has only one: Love. For me, Love summed up everything else. It was the one thing missing in my life. But why does God love me, I asked myself, even in my sins? Was I really so important to Him that He would pay the price for my sins? Allah is a God whose love is conditional. If I did something to displease him, he would not treat me with tenderness. Allah doesn't speak to the brokenness of his creatures — much less speak to his creatures directly, as the Christian God does.

And so, my desire for Christ grew. Whenever I picked up the Bible it was as if God were in direct conversation with me. Within minutes of reading, I would find passages that helped answer my questions. This was new to me: When I read the Koran, it was like going through a rule book, one full of hatred for non-Muslims. But the Bible is truly a living book, and it spoke to me.

For the first time in my life, I felt that I did not have to submit to Muslim law — which up to that point I had observed with great strictness — to come closer to God. Only when I met Jesus of Nazareth in the Bible did I realize that no law in the world, not even strict Sharia law, could make me just before God. Allah wanted me to submit to his rules; Jesus wanted me to love Him. And, more than that, Jesus wanted me to have faith in Him, to believe that He would make me just by His sacrifice, not through the violent means taught in the Hadith. Allah was a distant figure; Christ revealed His face. If I asked myself what God was really like, I didn't need an answer mediated by the mouth of a Prophet: God was present in the face of Jesus, and I was spellbound by His message.

I found that the God of the Bible was magnificent. It was the beginning of a personal revolution. I needed to know more. Each time I heard my mom snoring, I would take out the Bible from the hiding place in my room. I was extremely careful since I didn't even want to think about what my parents might do if they caught me.

I was fascinated by Jesus. He defended an adulteress and preached love and forgiveness for His enemies. I started to live by every word I read and wanted to know more about this unusual man. I remembered a film on Jesus that was always aired on TV at Easter. My parents switched the television off when the scene of the Crucifixion came.

"He was never crucified! The Christians only invented that," they said. But it was exactly this scene of someone being ready to sacrifice His life for the salvation of others that fascinated me most. I now wanted to watch the film to the end, so I ventured out into the city to try to buy a copy. But everywhere I went, my request was only met with snorts and chuckles. I was surprised because in the Muslim community, people who are interested in Islam are always helped. Everybody wants others to know Allah, but here no one really cared about Christ.

Suddenly I remembered something Joseph had told me: "Jesus lives, and He loves you!"

I thought, "Okay, Jesus, if you really are alive, then help me find this film!" When my next attempt was also fruitless, I gave up. It had become darker outside, so I headed home. As I sat disappointed on the tram, I felt like not even Jesus could help me.

"You are very pretty. Aren't you a singer?" I suddenly heard.

"No," I answered to the man sitting opposite me.

"Lady, I don't know why, but I have a feeling I must give you something," he continued.

"Well, it is Christmas soon! Give me a present," I joked sarcastically and smiled. The stranger handed me a flier that said: "Call this hotline and receive a free film about Jesus!" I never called the hotline, but I was deeply affected by this random meeting and was sure that once again, God had sent me an answer.

My heart was full of joy over this, but my head spoke to me with reason: "Sabatina, your parents are already infuriated that you don't want to marry Salman. How on earth will they react if you leave Islam? How will you live without your family?" I shuddered at the thought of losing them, and I knew that if I turned to Jesus that would be the end of my relationship with my family. Leaving Islam would be like committing suicide. I would be giving up my very identity. My whole life depended on it. And in addition, I would in effect sentence my parents and relatives to a life of suffering and shame, without even the ability to console them. Could I do such a terrible thing? Then it struck me: Maybe I could remain a Muslim on the outside but, in my heart, I could be a Christian and secretly go to church. This idea only lasted until my next furtive Bible reading, when I found, "Anyone who loves their father or mother more than me is not worthy of me," and "Whoever does not take up their cross and follow me is not worthy of me" (Matt. 10:37–38). Was I ready?

8

A Death Sentence

At the beginning of 2001, the situation at home was coming to a head. Hardly a day passed without my parents mentioning Salman and his visa. They simply couldn't understand that I didn't want him in Austria. This was about my life, a life that I wanted to live as a confident, independent, modern woman. During this period, I even began to reconsider a career in acting and sent some photos to a modeling agency. When my mother found the prints, she started to rage and shout that I was a whore.

If I were even five minutes late coming home, she yelled at me, "Who have you been lying with?" Of course, I had never slept with a man. But it was useless to try to convince her of that. Everything was exactly as it had been a year before, the only difference being that she no longer hit me. But these accusations and humiliations hurt much more than blows. I just wanted her to love me. I became increasingly lonely in my own home.

The more "Western" I became, the more my parents kept my sister Aisha away from me. My family was convinced that I was a bad influence on her. My two brothers simply did not understand why I made my mother cry and upset my father. They blamed me for destroying the family peace and making my parents suffer. I felt sorry for my parents because I knew their past and their hard struggles to build up a life for us in Austria. I knew that because I wouldn't get Salman a visa and behaved more like the Christian girls, the honor of my parents was being compromised. And I felt guilty for the tears my mother wept, but no one was interested in mine.

My parents showed love when I submitted. I longed to hug my mother, but unless I did what she wanted, I was only shown contempt. She saw me as her punishment from Allah. She would say, "Allah has punished me with you, but I have been doubly blessed with Aisha!" These words followed me to school and everywhere I went. My brothers and sister no longer spoke to me and threw me into absolute solitude. I wished we had stayed in Sarleinsbach and often thought back to the times when we had played together in the green meadows until it was dark outside. Just the thought of our happy life there would make me break down and cry.

One day, when we were fighting about my marriage to Salman, my father, livid with anger, leaned over our seventh-floor balcony and threatened to jump. He wanted to show that he would die of shame if I didn't get married. My mother continually forbade my brothers and sister to talk to me because I would not sign the marriage certificate. If gifts arrived from Pakistan, I wouldn't be given any, to punish me for not subjecting myself to the will of my parents. My situation seemed hopeless. I was now eighteen years old, and I had absolutely no idea how to find a way out.

I'd always tried to be a good Muslim, but now it had become clear that being a good Muslim meant forfeiting my freedom for family honor. I started to question that honor system. How was it honorable to live without a free will? I couldn't voice these questions; I'd been taught from a young age that no one can question Allah. But now I was reading the Bible almost every night and found that it was having an ever-greater impact on me. It seemed to radiate such peace and kindness — completely unlike Islam. Nevertheless, I forbade myself any further doubts about my own faith, even though I knew deep down that once I started on this path I couldn't turn back. The more I engaged with Jesus, the more absurd Muhammed appeared.

In the Koran, everything revolved around infidels and the superiority of Islam. The oppression of women and religious violence were legitimized and even encouraged.

Reading the Bible gave me a completely opposite vision. According to the Bible, I could not earn God's love. It was a gift already given to me and one that I could not repay, because Jesus Christ had paid for me with His death. The faith of which Jesus spoke was not measured by how often you prayed or through blind obedience to the rules written in the Koran. For the first time, I got to know a different God than Allah, one who gave me the right to call Him Father. Islam has no father, only a master of whom we are slaves. The God of the Bible was not angry about my clothes, nor did He force me into a suffocating code of honor. To this day, I find it liberating when I read: "People look at the outward appearance, but the Lord looks at the heart" (1 Sam. 16:7).

I was unfamiliar with this unconditional love; I knew it neither from Allah nor from my family, but I longed for it. Jesus loved everyone, not only the people that loved Him but also those who crucified Him. He could not do otherwise, for love was His nature. Whereas Islam excluded people — Jews, Christians, Hindus, atheists — Jesus spoke to the outcast and dined with sinners to save them. Jesus did not ask me to submit to Him like Allah did. Instead, He asked me to seek Him out and develop a relationship with Him and trust Him. I was moved and inspired by Him.

Soon enough I caught myself blaming Islam for my situation. And I was right. Only today, after extensively studying the teachings in the Hadith, have I realized that all the prohibitions and violence that I faced were not due to my parents' character but to the Sunna; that is, doing as the prophet Muhammed did. After all, Muhammed married a six-year-old when he was nearly fifty, so why would it be wrong to marry me as a sixteen-year-old? If my parents were practicing Christians, they would never force me to marry Salman as a matter of honor and religion. They would never have put me in a madrassa and abandoned me in Pakistan; they would never have tried to force me to live by values that simply didn't make sense in the Western world.

I wasn't just reading the Bible. A whole new world had opened before me, and I started reading other books about women who had left Islam.

Sometime during those nights when I lay in bed beside my sister and secretly read the Bible, I turned my back on Allah and his Prophet Muhammed. I no longer believed in them, or in the Koran, or in the superiority of Islam. The influence that my parents, my grandfather, and the imams at the madrassa had exerted over me for years was waning in favor of Jesus, the God who took a human face to save mankind. Even if no one in my family would ever understand it, I knew that I belonged to Jesus because I felt that I belonged to Love.

Suddenly it was easier for me to bear my situation. Instead of the fear of Allah's punishment or waiting for Paradise after death, a new desire was enkindled in me. After almost a year of studying the Bible and meeting Joseph, I was presented with a new way of living: the way of Truth and Love. I had never imagined that there was such a way to see the world, but in Christianity it was about loving God and His creatures. That was the highest demand. Christ's Kingdom was not an imaginary hereafter but was here on earth, wherever He is loved and where we love Him. I saw that there could be something like deliverance: a resurrection after death, where there will be justice, true justice — not the one that Sharia law demands, where the innocent suffer, but a paradise in which men and women are equal and where nobody is rewarded with seventy-two virgins (Al-Tirmidhi 1663 Sahih) because he has killed others in the name of Allah.

I wasn't harboring any illusions about the fact that converting to Christianity would only increase my problems. I'd been reading books where the authors described the persecution they suffered at the hands of their relatives after they converted. Those books were given to me by Joseph. How would my parents react when I told them that not only would I not marry Salman but that I had also become a Christian? They would insult me, beat me, disown me, and make me suffer however they could. And worst of all, I would lose them forever.

In the Gospel of Matthew, Jesus says, "The kingdom of heaven is like a merchant looking for fine pearls. When he found one of great value, he went away and sold everything he had and bought it" (13:45–46). The God of the Gospels was a God of challenge. He wanted to be taken seriously. He wanted to be my all or nothing — and nothing in between. That meant me valuing Him over my family, even over my own welfare. I had to ask myself honestly if He was worth all the suffering and risk. If He was truly the pearl of great price, then the sacrifice was mine to make.

In Pakistan, I used to light candles all over the house during Eid al-Fitr. I watched how the wax melted and the flame radiated a beautiful, warm light. Now Jesus had asked me to become a candle myself, to burn for Him by giving light to others through courage and at the cost of my own substance. He had asked me to die in order to live.

Burdened by this weight, I wanted to seek advice from someone who could help me to live out what Jesus was asking of me. I decided to go to a Catholic priest. I had always felt drawn to the Catholic Church, even though Joseph was Evangelical and I didn't really understand the differences between the denominations. Maybe it had something to do with my childhood in Sarleinsbach, where everyone was Catholic and extremely welcoming. In any case, when I arrived at the cathedral I marveled at the beauty of the architecture. Looking at a bowl of holy water, I went over and made some strange gestures — not the Sign of the Cross — that I thought approximated the washing ritual we performed before entering a mosque.

"How can I help you?" a friendly young man asked.

"I have a meeting with the pope!" I answered. He laughed. "The pope is not here, but I think I know where you want to go," he replied. He then brought me to the priest.

The priest had me sit in front of him on a chair. I could hardly wait to tell him about my newfound love and my experiences with Jesus. But after listening, he only stared at me and said, "It could be that Muhammed was also a prophet. We do not know!" It seemed that he was more interested in defending Islam than welcoming me into the Church. He didn't even offer to baptize me. I thought maybe he never had experienced anything with Jesus or that he was completely naive. The priest did not even offer to help in case I had to flee from my family. I was discouraged. I had taken a great risk to go into a Catholic church, and the minister of Christ had just sent me away.

So I went back to the Evangelicals. At least they honored the words of Jesus, who said: "No one comes to the Father except through me" (John 14:6). I had known enough of Muhammed to be certain that he, contra the priest, was not a way to the Father.

Soon after, I met Joseph in a restaurant. We often skipped school to talk about God. I told him about my meeting with the priest and that it had not deterred me: I wanted to follow Jesus in my own life. He couldn't believe it at first, but then he was so happy that he could hardly eat his meal. He started to pray with me. Right then I officially confessed that Jesus was my Lord who died for my sins to give me eternal life. I accepted that I was a sinner who needed Him. I invited Him to dwell in my heart.

We were so excited that we left without paying the bill. Our waiter came running after us. We were so sorry and utterly embarrassed. But also filled with joy. I had no idea then what the power of the gospel would do to me.

One day, after arriving back home, my mother confronted me with an ultimatum: Sign the marriage certificate or face the consequences. In my heart I knew that my family would disown me for my decision for Jesus, and that Jesus wanted me to choose Him before any other person in this world — even if they were my own flesh and blood. Trusting in His guidance, without knowing where to go, I said to my mother that day that I did not want to sign the certificate and marry Salman.

Then I was shocked at my own words. How could I be saying this? It was obvious what this meant, and my mother's look told me that she knew it as well. This was the end.

We stared at each other. It was spectrally quiet. My mother's cheeks were glowing with rage and her eyelids were flickering.

She went into my room, wrenched open the closet, and dragged everything out. Then she came back, opened the front door, and threw everything in her hands out into the hallway. Finally, she snatched up an empty plastic bag and threw it out into the hall as well.

Among the other insults, the one that I remember to this day was: "If I had known that you would turn out like this, I would have killed you when you were an infant!"

She pushed me out into the hallway and slammed the door shut in my face. I stood there as if turned to stone. Not a single tear. It was over.

Then I tried to push the button to call the elevator, but my hands were shaking, and I was so weak that I couldn't even call the elevator.

The first thing I did was walk over to my siblings' school to say goodbye to them. I didn't have a plan. All I had was a plastic bag full of random clothing. The last gift of my mother. I didn't even know where I was going to sleep that night. I was homeless. Apart from Joseph, with whom I most certainly couldn't spend the night, I had hardly any friends. My only choice was to go to the youth homeless shelter. It wasn't ideal, but it was a place to start.

The two counselors who had been in charge of my case the last time were on duty when I arrived at the homeless shelter. I told them everything that had happened and they immediately agreed to take me in. I settled into a small room beneath the roof while the counselors called my parents to inform them that I was safe and would be staying at the shelter. I started to look for work and a more permanent place to stay.

Looking for a job made me realize how unprepared and unqualified I was. I'd been working since I got back from Pakistan but hadn't saved anything. Since I had experience working in a café, I began presenting myself to café owners around town asking if they needed any help.

After some time in the homeless shelter, there was an opening in a residence sponsored by a Protestant church group. The room they provided for me had only enough space for a narrow bed, a table, a wardrobe, a bookcase, and a small kitchenette. The toilet and shower were down the hall. It was tiny. And there was a problem: I was hungry and there was nothing to eat. In the homeless shelter, at least we were provided meals.

Now I was sitting in front of an empty fridge. Not a single piece of bread. I started to cry and, opening the Bible to turn to Jesus, my eyes fell on this passage:

> Look at the birds of the air; they do not sow or reap or store away in barns, and yet your heavenly Father feeds them. Are you not much more valuable than they? Can any one of you by worrying add a single hour to your life?
>
> And why do you worry about clothes? See how the flowers of the field grow. They do not labor or spin. Yet I tell you that not even Solomon in all his splendor was dressed like one of these. If that is how God clothes the grass of the field, which is here today and tomorrow is thrown into the fire, will he not much more clothe you — you of little faith? So do not worry, saying, "What shall we eat?" or "What shall we drink?" or "What shall we wear?" For the pagans run after all these things, and your heavenly Father knows that you need them. But seek first his kingdom and his righteousness, and all these things will be given to you as well. (Matt. 6:26–33)

After reading these verses, I was still hungry, but I trusted God. Moreover, I had trained my body to not eat or drink during Ramadan. Now at least there was water.

And then I received a call. The homeless shelter wanted me to come over. One of the girls who bullied me there and had stolen my money before I moved asked for forgiveness. Then she came in with a huge box of all my favorite foods. It seemed to me that it was coming directly from God. "This girl will pay back every penny she has stolen," the counselor said. But I forgave her. To please my God who had not forgotten my needs, I decided to forget what she had done to me.

I started to work, and I studied and met Joseph and his church members regularly. For almost an entire month I didn't hear from my parents. They seemed to be leaving me in peace. I was eighteen years old and living my first summer of freedom. To celebrate this, I did what any young girl does when she wants to prove her independence and show everyone that she is her own woman: I dyed my hair. Even the most mundane things, like going to McDonald's or buying groceries, were exciting for me.

While I was making friends, working, and enjoying my new life, I was also exploring my newfound faith with zeal. I spent lots of time reading the Bible and talking to Joseph about God. I went to an Evangelical church and Bible study and was quickly accepted into this religious community, one totally unlike the one I had left. The other members of my church and the people in my Bible study group enabled me to explore what Christianity meant for me and my life. They were kind and supportive rather than strict and cruel. I wasn't reprimanded for asking questions but encouraged. If I didn't understand something we read, we discussed it and evaluated how we could apply the tenets of the Bible to our own lives. In my new faith, I found the unconditional love I'd been craving my entire life. Finally, I felt part of a community that valued me as a member and respected my individuality.

My new life was going great. I was making my own decisions and learning to live on my own. I even had a boyfriend, one whom I didn't have to hide or lie about, a boyfriend I could be seen with in public. I met Tarek when I had been searching for a job; he managed the café where I sometimes picked up shifts.

I thought he was strikingly handsome and wonderful. His father was Tunisian, so he understood what it was like to come from a Muslim family, but his mother was Austrian. He himself wasn't religious. I appreciated that he understood the world I'd grown up in, but didn't live the rules of Muhammed as in the world I'd just escaped from. He was older than I was, which meant he understood how to live on his own and helped me negotiate my newfound independence. He was always scolding me for being too friendly to strangers. Every time we left each other he would say, "Bye, Sabatina; don't talk to too many people!"

I did anyway, though. In fact, not a day went by when I didn't meet someone new. I was so curious about the world and hungry for friendship. And I wanted everyone to know about Jesus. I even joined a street evangelization group, but when only young men stopped to "hear about Jesus," my colleagues thought it was better I do a different sort of evangelization — whatever that meant. I was surprised that no one else was speaking about Jesus. I had discovered a great truth, and through it, freedom, and I wanted everyone to know it.

This period of exploration and awakening was to last just six weeks. I finally got a call from my parents. At first, I was happy to hear from them, as I hadn't spoken to them since our family meeting at the shelter. Now that I had my own apartment, the counselors at the homeless shelter were no longer in contact with my parents. They were no longer responsible for me, though I could still reach out for advice. As much as I was enjoying my new life, I missed them. My father was particularly pleasant. He urged me to come home but didn't push it further when I refused.

A few days later he called again and announced that he was coming to visit me in my new home. It was unexpected, and I couldn't help but be apprehensive. When he arrived, he was friendly and charming, but he quickly turned the conversation to me coming home, which was no surprise. But now that he was sitting opposite me in person, he wouldn't be brushed off so easily.

"You have to come home. It's a matter of honor," he insisted.

"I can't, Father."

"Do you still not know what's right?"

I saw that he was starting to lose patience, but I wasn't afraid of him.

"Yes, I do know what's right. And what you're asking me to do isn't right. It is not right to marry a man I don't love. It is not right to live under oppression. That's not what God says."

"What God, Sabatina, what God are you talking about?" There was no turning back now. I gathered all my courage.

"I don't believe in the same God as you, Father. I believe in Jesus Christ."

I had barely gotten the words out when he stormed out of the apartment without looking back.

I wasn't sure how I should feel about my confession. My heart was pounding, but I was glad that I'd told my father the truth. I couldn't hide my God behind a veil. He had become my everything. But I knew exactly what the penalty was for converting to Christianity, and I also knew only too well just how much value my parents placed on Islam. At the same time though, I couldn't imagine that they would really do anything to me. I knew I'd hurt them deeply, but they were my parents. And this was Austria, not Pakistan. Even though my parents lived according to Sharia law, people didn't just go around stoning women to death.

While I understood the potential consequences, I also knew I had no choice. I hadn't told my father to provoke him or to rebel against his demands. I told him because this was who I was: a Christian. I didn't have a choice in the matter. If I were still a believing Muslim, perhaps I could have submitted, but I wasn't. The life he lived and wanted me to live was no longer mine, so his decisions for me didn't apply.

Only a few hours after my father had left my apartment, I received a phone call from my mother. In no uncertain terms, she made it clear how deeply she hated me. In her eyes, I was as low as every other Austrian whore. Their words stung, but my parents had been calling me these names for years. I had a newfound strength — it would take a lot more than a few phone calls to break my spirit. And I was sure they would come around. They might never fully accept it, but they'd adjust. They couldn't terrorize me forever.

Over the next few days, the barrage of calls continued, and I did my best to endure them. I went to school, worked, and met Joseph. I felt safe with him; for the first time in my life, I had someone I could really talk to. And in spite of my parents' angry phone calls, I still felt relatively safe. I knew that they were hurt and offended by my change of faith, but I couldn't imagine that they would do anything worse than give me a beating, and since I didn't live at home, it wasn't like they could get their hands on me. It never occurred to me that they might try to kill me. I was their daughter, and I firmly believed that the ties that bound us together as a family were stronger than their faith and honor.

Sometimes my father came to my apartment and stationed himself in front of the door, banging on it and shouting. If I didn't open it, he would disappear again after a while and I was left in tears.

One day he even appeared at the café where I worked, ranting and raging for so long that I fled to the bathroom and locked myself inside. It was only with great difficulty that my boss was able to persuade him to leave the café. Naturally, after being the cause of such a scene, I was fired.

The situation was getting out of control. I hadn't worked at the café long enough to have any real savings. I urgently needed money, but I was afraid my father would make another scene if I found a new job. No, this had gone on long enough. I would have to talk to him and make him understand.

Despite all that my mother and father had done, despite the decisions I had made that had distanced me from them, they were still the most important people in the world to me. Although I showed a stoic face, their insults hurt me deeply. Christian or not, I was their daughter. When they rejected me, I couldn't just accept it and walk away. Something would have been missing. And although I'd found belonging in Christ, the church couldn't fill the void of no longer being a part of my family.

I tried so hard. Some of my Austrian friends couldn't bear hearing my family problems and thought I should just cut off all contact with them. But I couldn't; it wasn't how I was raised. In Pakistan, the family and the community are the heart of the social order, and children spend the majority of their time within the family. When you spend eighteen years of your lifetime not just in the same house but in the same room, there is a closeness and bond that is unparalleled in Western families. The importance of guarding the family honor is drilled into every child. The rights of the individual do not count. Individual rights are not self-evident; this is a Christian concept.

Though I'd changed, my family was still a major part of me. It went beyond the violence and abuse. It was a bond so deep that it couldn't be broken. Cutting off contact just wasn't an option. And it was the strength of this bond that led me to meet them at home, certain that they wouldn't actually do anything serious.

In the early afternoon of June 2, 2001, I entered my parents' apartment. I hadn't wanted to go alone, but none of my friends were willing to come with me except a family friend who was also a Pakistani. As it turned out, it wasn't going to be just a family affair. My parents had also asked Ahmed to be there. This would be a difficult conversation; we all knew that. The atmosphere was so hostile that my mother didn't even offer chai to her guests, which was absolutely unheard of in Pakistani culture.

We went into the living room. I had hardly sat down when another guest entered: Salman. I felt the world spinning. Hadn't I left him behind in Pakistan? Hadn't I refused to get him a visa? My father saw the look on my face and calmly told me that since I'd refused to sign the marriage certificate, he and my mother had adopted Salman as their son so that they could get him a visa to come to Austria.

He looked at me without speaking and sat down beside Ahmed. My father asked me whether this story about Christianity was a lie, a new excuse to get out of marrying Salman.

"The Bible has convinced me that Christianity is superior to Islam," I answered.

Horrified, my mother leapt out of her chair at me, but my father held her back.

"You know what will happen to you according to our religion, don't you? One day you will go to Hell!" she yelled.

I stood up disappointed. There was no point. This meeting was not going to make anything better. As I was about to leave the room, Ahmed spoke up.

"Sabatina, are you quite sure that you are a Christian?" I nodded while feelings of fear cropped up within me.

"You know what will happen to you according to our religion, don't you?"

I remained silent. I knew what happens in Islam when you leave it.

"Normally you would have three days to reconsider," he said.

In Islamic law, particularly within the Shafi'i school, apostates are given a brief but severe window to repent, often lasting up to three days. During this time, they are not simply urged to reconsider their decision; they are often imprisoned and subjected to torture until they come back to Islam. This window is not just a formality — it is a final, unyielding chance to return to the ummah, a chance to reconcile with the faith before irrevocable consequences ensue. If the apostate fails to repent, the ultimate penalty — execution — awaits. This is what my father and Ahmed were referencing: a chilling reality, the consequences of apostasy both clear and unforgiving.

In Islam, apostasy is viewed as a sin so grave that it is punishable by death, a reality that makes conversion to Christianity in the Muslim world a rare act. Those who do convert often conceal their faith, terrified of the unimaginable consequences that await if their decision is exposed. In some countries, the death penalty is sanctioned through the legal system; in others, it is enforced by ruthless mob violence. While some argue that the death sentence should be carried out without hesitation, others insist that the accused should face trial in a Muslim legal tribunal. Yet, across every interpretation, one conclusion is inevitable: Despite disagreements over the details, Muslim scholars, united in this, agree that the apostate must die.

"We will give you two weeks," Ahmed continued.

Meanwhile, he folded his hands and without looking at me threatened: "Please, don't force us to do what we'll have to do otherwise."

To me, the threat came so suddenly and so unexpectedly that I simply stood there, paralyzed. Salman, who hadn't said a word the entire time, walked over and stood in front of the door.

I was numb and confused, my mind reeling as I tried to piece together what they had just said. I couldn't believe it. The words refused to sink in. Were they just trying to scare me into coming back? How could they actually talk about killing me? But I also knew how seriously they took the words of the Prophet Muhammed. As I looked at my mother and Abba, I saw that they were serious: My parents and Ahmed had just threatened to kill me for my faith.

9

Resisting the Ummah

I HADN'T GONE to the police before because I knew that the Muslim community did not play by Austrian rules. It wouldn't have helped my case: Going outside the community was an affront to family honor. It meant I didn't trust them or value their belief system. But now everything was different. With some encouragement from Tarek, I reported the incident to the police.

When I arrived at the police station, I told the officer that my parents, who were Muslim, had threatened to kill me because I'd converted to Christianity. The policeman looked at me with a blank expression. He didn't seem to think I was serious.

"Why don't you just convert back to Islam?" he asked me.

I didn't know how I was supposed to tell this man my story if he already didn't believe me. I would have to start at the beginning. For the next hour I described everything: the fights with my parents over my integration into Western culture, my time in Pakistan, the forced engagement, the beatings, how I'd finally run away and converted.

When I finished, the officer seemed satisfied that according to the law, they had threatened me and held me against my will. He told me they would arrest my father. I couldn't believe it — that wasn't what I was trying to accomplish at all. What would my family do if my father were arrested? My mother would never be able to support the family on her own and my siblings would be devastated.

"I don't want you to arrest anyone," I said. "I just want you to protect me."

The police didn't know what to do with me. One moment I wanted them to protect me, the next I was trying to protect my parents. What they didn't understand was that it wasn't a choice between being afraid of my parents or loving them. It was both. I couldn't bear to bring more shame on my family by sending them to prison, but I was also terrified that they would do what they had said they would do. I had come to the police because I thought they would protect me and because I had a right to be safe. But I was also torn by my emotions, and there was no room for that within the law. The police officer made it clear that he couldn't offer me protection unless there had been a real physical attempt.

I cried out that I would kill myself if they arrested my father, and he called the police psychologist to evaluate me, who determined that I was mentally sound and not a threat to myself. I was told to go home and that they would be in touch within a few days after they'd had a chance to talk to my parents.

I didn't dare go back to my apartment because I didn't know if my father might already be there waiting for me. The police had abandoned me. I turned to Joseph, who agreed to meet me close to his apartment.

When I arrived, there was no trace of him. The corner where we'd agreed to meet was directly in front of Razia's family's house, and I was terrified that someone might see me and tell my parents where I was. I was completely lost. Should I go to my parents, ask for their forgiveness, and claim that I was a good Muslim? Tell them that my conversion had only been a pretense? Tell them that I might even be ready to marry Salman? I couldn't. I couldn't lie. I couldn't do this to Jesus. I couldn't go back, but I was afraid of what would happen if I didn't. I had no way out.

After forty-five minutes, Joseph still hadn't shown up.

"I'm sorry, Sabatina. I can't come. It's too dangerous," he said when I called. "Take care of yourself."

I was devastated but I also understood him. To my parents, Joseph was evil incarnate. But I was also jealous of his situation. We were the same age and close friends, but Joseph had something I would never have. His parents were supportive and protective of him, while mine were threatening to hurt me for leaving their faith. The fact that Joseph didn't come made it more real than ever. After that, the only one I could rely on was Jesus.

When I'd left my parents' home, I thought I was opening a new chapter in my life, one filled with faith, freedom, and possibility. I thought I'd found a religion that offered me unconditional love and a community that supported me even when I made mistakes. But I was hardly an adult, and I was realizing that I had vastly underestimated the consequences of my conversion. I naively thought my parents would find a way to forgive me and we could somehow become a family again. But my parents would never be content unless I returned to them, and I knew I'd never be able to live with myself if I went back to Islam. I'd broken their trust, insulted their faith, and destroyed their honor.

Since Joseph couldn't be there for me, I called Tarek and asked him to meet me. When he arrived, Tarek criticized Joseph for abandoning me — they'd never gotten along — and said he thought Joseph was being a coward.

But in truth, neither Joseph or Tarek could really help me. I had never felt so alone. Everyone I cared about seemed to be pulling me in a different direction.

The next two weeks were a blur. I'm not sure how I made it through them. I practically barricaded myself in my apartment. I supported myself with food tickets that were given out to homeless people. Anytime anyone spoke to me it was like I was underwater. I could go through the motions, but I didn't really process what anyone was saying.

I heard nothing from my family during this time. A few days later, the police called me back in to testify formally to what I'd said the night of the threat. I told them not to go ahead with the investigation as I didn't want to harm my parents. So the police went to interview my parents, a process that took two weeks, before calling me to come back again.

My family denied everything. My mother explained that they wanted me to come home because I was psychologically unbalanced. And, in their eyes, that wasn't a lie: In Islam, the only comprehensible reason for leaving Islam is insanity. My parents could see no reason other than insanity for leaving their faith. I know that my parents truly believed that I had gone crazy and wanted me to come back so that they could protect me from myself. There was no room in their worldview for a change of faith; they couldn't fathom that I had rationally chosen Christ over Muhammed. They were worried about my spiritual safety: Until I came back to Islam, I was guaranteed to burn in Hell for eternity. By trying to bring me back to them, they were saving my soul.

The police told me there was nothing more they could do. I came to them claiming that my father was trying to kill me but broke down when they mentioned arresting him. Then, when they said they could do nothing, I begged them to protect me from my family. In their eyes it was irrational behavior, and they had no context for understanding Muslim culture and the pressures my parents and I were under.

Meanwhile, the community of believers, the ummah, did its best to make my life miserable. The ummah works like a series of concentric circles, all of them exerting pressure on an individual to stay within the boundaries of Islam and the community. The innermost circle is the immediate family, followed by the extended family, close family friends, and then the community as a whole. All these different groups were connected to me and had a vested interest in bringing me back to Islam. I was being watched and criticized from all sides. Some of them spit on me while passing by. Others taunted me with derogatory names. I could feel it palpably: Eventually something was going to explode.

All my friends told me to get out of Linz, which, as I have said, is a small city where it wasn't difficult to find me. My parents and their friends eventually found out where I was working or got their hands on my cell phone number. Once they had my number, my parents and their friends would call and insult me incessantly. Everyone had an opinion, and everyone felt responsible for bringing me back to the ummah. Some people would threaten and insult me. Others would use kindness to take advantage of my vulnerability.

Once, a member of Razia's family wanted to meet, so I agreed to see him in a café. He asked me to come back to Islam, and when I refused, he sexually harassed me. Another man seeking to bring me back into the fold poured a large amount of alcohol into my drink, thinking that he could rape me after I blacked out. But since I had never drunk alcohol before, I discovered the ruse immediately and ran out of the bar. He followed and tried to kiss me. Afterward, his wife called me and said, "Are the Austrians not enough for you that you have to come after our men?"

As I had always done, I grabbed onto anyone who showed me kindness or affection. One was Jamal, a man who in the past had stood up for me. I thought I could trust him because he was married to an Austrian woman and he also had a relationship with my family. We used to go out for long drives and talk about what I was going through, and it was a relief to have a good listener on my side. One day we were on one of our drives when he went farther out of Linz than we'd ever been before. I had no idea where we were going.

Suddenly he pulled over by a river and looked at me intently. He wanted to kiss me. I'd never be able to fight him off, and even if I could, where would I go? The only thing around us was the forest. My mind raced as he told me that he loved me, that he'd always loved me, and that we could run away and be together and nobody would ever find us. He told me he hated Tarek and would kill him for taking me away from him. I knew I couldn't panic or risk upsetting him. Thinking quickly, I told him in my most innocent and calming voice that I returned his feelings, but we couldn't do this there. I still had my family issues to work out, and he had his wife, and running away simply wasn't an option. It simply wasn't right for us to give in to our passions. Somehow my persuasion worked. He started the car and drove me back home. I never spoke to Jamal again.

I learned an important lesson from that encounter: As a Muslim woman I had a low status. As a Christian, I had no status all. Any Muslim man could do anything to me and there would be no moral consequences (a lot I share with many Christian women in Muslim countries). In Austria it was hard to describe the parallel society built by Muslims. All these men who harassed me were married. They looked perfectly integrated. Many of them had high-paying jobs. Some owned restaurants. Others worked in offices. All worked together to keep their parallel society intact, and when their efforts to bring me back to Islam didn't work, they tried to drug me and sexually exploit me.

The insults from the ummah were both relentless and unexpected. One afternoon I was walking down the street when I saw an old friend with his two daughters. Many times, my family had gone to his house to break the fast during Ramadan. I hadn't seen them for some time and was excited to catch up with them. I waved and ran across the street to greet them, but our family friend backed away, pulling his daughters with him. As he turned them around to walk in the opposite direction, I saw him tug on his belt and hear him say to his daughters, "Her father doesn't have one strong enough to keep her in line." I was horrified at the violence and animosity directed at me. I had thought only my family would go so far as to threaten me, but everyone I knew seemed to take it upon themselves to harass me.

I could barely walk down the street without being followed by jeers, and my phone didn't stop ringing with the voices of angry friends on the other end. On the street, the insults only became worse. At first it was people I knew, but when an Iraqi man I hardly knew walked up to me on the street, called me a whore, spat on me, and walked away, I was terrified at how widespread the shunning had become.

I fluctuated between fear, sadness, and denial. It was torture, but where should I have gone? Even the Catholic Church, which I had sought out in the beginning, had sent me away. I wanted everyone to understand. So many times, I had tried to tell my mother and father what Salman had done to me in Pakistan, how he had sexually abused me night after night, but they wouldn't hear it. My mother always changed the subject when I tried to tell her why I wouldn't marry him. My father silenced me, unwilling to listen to anything I had to say that was at odds with what he wanted for me. I needed to be heard, and I couldn't leave Linz until I had accomplished that.

I was so overwhelmed with trying to lay low while also continuing to make a life for myself that I dropped out of school and began working full-time. Despite everything that was going on, I was doing well professionally. I took a job as a secretary but convinced my boss to let me join the sales team. Soon enough, without any training or experience, I was the company's top seller. My boss was so impressed he asked me if I would be interested in training new hires in the company, which I immediately accepted. I was thrilled: This meant more responsibility and frequent travel to offices in other cities.

When my parents found out what I was doing, as they inevitably did through their network, things quickly fell apart. In their view, staying in hotels was something only prostitutes did, and there was no reason why I would have a job that sent me to cities all over Austria. They were appalled and started tracking me down whenever I was away from Linz. They were also unable to understand that I could be supporting myself, and assumed I used my job as a ruse to cover the fact that I was a kept woman or a prostitute. One time my mother called the hotel where I was staying and asked if I was in my room. The receptionist said yes, that I'd just arrived and had gone upstairs with a man. My mother called my room and began screaming at me, calling me a bitch, a whore, every horrible name she could think of. It didn't matter that the man in question was the taxi driver, and he was simply helping me carry my bags up. It was enough to convince her that I was living in sin like a Christian.

My father went to my boss and told him I was a disgrace to the family honor. His tactics might have worked in Pakistan, but here the boss didn't care what I did in my free time. My parents were relentless; they were trying to destroy every area of my life to convince me I couldn't survive on my own. My boss thankfully didn't heed my father's charming appearance or his threats, but the fact that my father had pursued him was worrying enough.

The one constant I had in my life was Jesus. When Joseph gave me the Bible, I read it the way he used to read it: I skipped the Old Testament and went straight to the Gospels and the stories of Jesus. And I had joined Joseph's Evangelical church, a small congregation on the outskirts of town.

As a child, I had been taught that the highest honor was dying as a martyr for Allah, and now I saw how cruel and destructive that worldview was. In Islam, a martyr is someone who inflicts violence on others to spread the mission. In Christianity a martyr is someone like Jesus, ready to die for the salvation of mankind. Christianity was neither a mathematical formula nor a set of rules in a book, but a relationship to Truth, who is a Person. Unlike Allah, its God is forgiving and accepting. And He told me to love my enemy, so I did: I prayed for my family all the time.

Not only did I pray for them, I pursued them as well. I would change my number as soon as they found out what it was, but after a few weeks, missing them desperately, I would call them and try to work things out. It was a cycle of pulling away and coming back, none of us able to permanently break the bonds between us.

Everything kept escalating the longer I stayed in Linz, yet I continued to be ignored by the authorities. Anytime I went to them explaining that I'd been threatened, they looked at me skeptically. Nobody believed anything so extreme could happen in Linz; nobody considered that there might be Muslims who placed Sharia law above Austrian law. I was disenchanted with the bureaucracy, with the unwillingness of the police to protect me when it was clear I was being threatened. I think their attitude probably also led me to underestimate the gravity of the situation. If the police weren't going to take me seriously, did I really have anything to worry about? I honestly didn't know if my parents would ever do what they said they would; after all, they hadn't made any physical threats so far. All I wanted was to live in peace, and I told myself if I didn't respond to their insults and accusations, eventually they would give up. So I turned to my new faith and tried to ignore the warning signs that the situation was far more serious than the police believed.

One evening, out of the blue, my phone rang.

"It's me, your husband." It was Salman.

Horrified, I hung up. Immediately I knew something was going on. I hadn't heard from him in months, but all of a sudden he called and referred to himself as my husband.

Shortly afterward I received a call from city hall saying I should come down, as there was something to clear up. I was speechless when I arrived and discovered that my parents had filed a marriage certificate for Salman and me.

"This certificate was issued by the Pakistani authorities and has been certified by the Austrian embassy in Islamabad," the woman at the registry office told me. "Once the paperwork goes through, it will be official."

I was dumbfounded. It was an obvious forgery. I hadn't married Salman in Pakistan; we'd only had the engagement ceremony. No official had been present, and I had not signed anything. When the woman showed me my signature on the marriage certificate, I protested that it wasn't mine. She was taken aback by my reaction. She had called me in as a matter of protocol, not expecting me to claim it was a forgery. She told me that despite my claim, the registration would likely go through, given that in Pakistan a woman doesn't have to be present at her own marriage. Islamic law permits the *wali*, the guardian, to marry for the woman, even if she is not present.

Furthermore, the Austrian embassy there had been thorough: Salman, his parents, and all the neighbors had been questioned, and they had all said that the marriage had taken place. My lone statement meant nothing; there was nobody to corroborate my story. It was that simple. I had to accept it. Without having signed or done anything, I was married to a man whom I rejected with all my being. Before I left, the woman said she'd file a report but didn't think it would do much good.

Everyone in the community knew that I hadn't signed the marriage certificate. It was clear that my father had forged my name, and that Salman and his family had been lying when they said there had been a wedding in Pakistan. The only people who didn't know, or didn't care to know, were the Austrian authorities. I hoped it was only a formality, that my family had only done this so they could get Salman a visa.

Hardly a day went by without angry and insulting phone calls from my family, demanding that I come back and live with my husband. When I failed to react, they invented ever-new reasons why I should return home. They told me that my grandfather was ill and was going blind. Then they claimed that my uncle was dying. Of course, I was to blame for all of this. The shame I'd brought on the family had driven everyone to despair.

Salman, above all, called me constantly and harassed me. He was frustrated that I wouldn't stay with him, even with the marriage certificate, and jealous of anyone else I spent time with. He took to stalking me and threatening me physically; he called me constantly and brought me to previously unknown depths of fear.

"Where are you?" he shouted over the phone. "I'll find you, and if you don't come with me, you'll pay for it."

Things were getting continuously worse. Salman had been following my movements. I was at an amusement park near Linz one day with a friend of mine when my phone rang.

"Who are you with? I can see him! Who is he?" Salman screamed at me. I spun around, trying to find him in the crowd of people. I couldn't see him, but he could see me, and he could see who I was with. I was trying to enjoy a carefree day with a friend and Salman had found me. Fear was taking over my life; I knew I couldn't live like this anymore.

My relationship with Tarek came to an end because of the stress of my situation. I still saw Joseph, but I hadn't told him about the marriage. There was only one way out of my situation: I would have to cut all ties, leave Linz, and start a new life where nobody could find me. But I was prevented by the fact that I had nowhere to go. I didn't know anyone in any other city, and I had no idea how far my parents' influence stretched. How far would I have to go to remain safe? And while I lived in fear, the idea of leaving terrified me still more. I was still naive enough to believe that eventually everyone would calm down, my parents would accept my decisions, and Salman would move on with his life. I missed my family, I missed being part of the ummah, and cutting myself off completely was still too bleak to contemplate.

On Saturday, June 15, 2002, the decision was made for me. It was early morning, and I was still in bed when my phone rang. I still don't know why I picked up, but I did. Salman's voice immediately brought me to consciousness.

"You accursed, miserable slut, you have my father on your conscience!" he screamed into the phone.

"Salman, what's happened?" I tried to make my voice sound calm.

"You know exactly, you slut. He's dead. Of grief, because you won't live with me. You killed him and you're going to pay for it!"

During the previous weeks, my parents had mentioned several times that Salman's father wasn't well. They blamed me for his illness, but I hadn't taken them seriously — I thought it was like all the other stories they had made up to get me to come home.

"Salman," I said, "Calm down. I didn't kill him and you know it. He was sick."

"My father is dead, and he's dead because you're not living with me. You killed him! You won't live to see tomorrow!"

I hung up the phone. I had never heard him like this before. I knew he was bad, but now he sounded capable of anything. The death of his father had left him completely unhinged, and my conversion to Christianity would give him all the more reason to carry it out. I knew I wasn't safe, and I couldn't afford to wait around. I packed up my few belongings and left Linz.

Joseph's church members brought me to a farm outside the town. But I couldn't stay there long. The man who ran the farm was handicapped and was himself relying on his family. Also, it was still too close to Linz.

I was in shock. Even though I rationally should have known where this all might lead, when it actually happened — when I left my hometown and my family for fear of my life — I felt orphaned and rejected. I wasn't in a state to do much of anything, including properly care for myself.

I knew I couldn't stay with them in the countryside forever. I was as shut off from the world as I had been in my tiny apartment in Linz. I had traded one hiding place for another, but I wasn't living my life. If there was one thing I had learned, it was that I didn't want to spend my life in fear. I still had dreams of becoming an actress or singer; and besides, I couldn't depend on the generosity of others forever. I needed a place where I could both be anonymous and be myself.

Vienna was the obvious choice. It was a large city where I could blend in, and I knew a few people there who could help me get settled. When I left, I took with me nothing more than a few clothes, some makeup, my cell phone, and what little money I had saved up over the past two years.

The train ride was only two hours, but it felt endless. I spent the entire time thinking about how my mother had thought of Salman as her new son. She had favored him over me, her own daughter. I felt jealousy and pain resurface and focused on the landscape flashing past the window.

I couldn't let myself grow distracted by my emotions. I had to stay alert. I observed any non-European passenger on the train with suspicion. I knew all too well that news in the Pakistani community travels faster than sound, and I feared that my family might have already sent someone to bring me back. That they could not possibly know my plans didn't even cross my mind — I was on the run, and everyone was a potential spy.

A woman I met through Joseph had given me the address of a Christian church in Vienna where I could knock on the door and be able to stay for a couple of nights. When I finally arrived, I called Milena, a model I had met in Linz. She was a few years older than me, with long hair and even longer legs. I told her about my past and that I was looking for work so I could build a new life in Vienna.

"I know a famous photographer," she told me. "I think he'll find you incredibly sexy and could take some photos of you for a portfolio. Working with him is a real privilege." She gave me his phone number and told me to simply give him a call and say she'd recommended him. His name was Peter Baumann.

In my current position, with no perspective or even the belief that I could make it on my own, I was immediately sold on this idea. Whenever anyone offered to help me, I blindly followed their instructions. I trusted everyone and took everyone at their word. I didn't stop to think about what kind of help people were offering, nor what it would cost me down the line. It was just about survival, as I was basically homeless again. Peter Baumann was an impressive photographer, and if Milena sent me to him, I would do what she said. It never occurred to me that he would take advantage of my vulnerability. I didn't even think I was vulnerable. I had learned to be skeptical of the members of the Pakistani community, but I didn't want to bring my old fears into my new life. For me every Austrian was another Christian. Muslims don't differentiate between practicing or non-practicing Christians, and since I was so new to the faith and not even baptized, how should I have known that there are people that are baptized and take their faith seriously — and then there are people like Baumann. Those offering help knew about my miserable situation, so I assumed they would just want to support me. I couldn't have been more wrong.

I called Baumann and went over to meet him that same day in the late afternoon. At the time, Baumann, who has since died, lived in an upscale neighborhood of Vienna. Milena had not said much, only that he had a great reputation and that he shot for big magazines. He had even photographed Miss World, which impressed me the most and rekindled my childhood dream of becoming an actress or singer.

When Baumann opened the door, I was confronted by a man who was not at all what I expected: His hands were shaking and he was clearly drunk — a blend of green tea and vodka, as it turned out. His long, narrow face was red, wrinkled, and bloated at the same time; he had a white, stubbly beard; and his hair was an undefinable color and tied back in a greasy ponytail. But he was by no means rude and, despite his drunken state, he was still a charmer.

He smiled kindly and led me into a room that probably served as a studio as well as bedroom and living room — I tried not to pay attention to the chaos of his apartment, which I presumed was a sign of eccentric genius.

He started the conversation, "You're a beautiful girl, and I can already imagine what I can do with you." He spoke with a thick Viennese accent and peppered his conversation with phrases I wasn't familiar with, but I knew were not very polite. "But you do realize that in order to make it in this business, you'll need to spread your legs."

"Yes, of course," I replied. "Spread your legs" — the way he said it, I thought he just meant I would have to learn to pose. Of course, I eagerly agreed; I had no idea what he really meant.

He burst into a fit of laughter. "I like you. I tell you to spread your legs and you say 'of course.' Unbelievable!"

His amusement irritated me. I knew he was laughing at me, but I didn't know why. I told myself it must be all those green tea cocktails, and we made an appointment for him to take some photos.

When I showed up at the appointed time, his hands weren't trembling as much. He showed me how I should look in front of the camera, and I did exactly what he told me. The poses were provocative, but I was never completely naked. Baumann told me to look "wicked." Again, I wasn't sure what he wanted, but I didn't question him because I simply assumed this is what one did in "the business."

I liked some of the photos Baumann took, but only a few, and they did get me appointments with other photographers, just like he'd promised. In order to get actual paying jobs, I would need to put together a portfolio with a selection of shots from different photographers. They were delighted that I was so willing to take revealing photos. It never occurred to me to say no. I was just happy to be making a career and some new friends.

I felt very accepted in this world. In Pakistan, my teachers tried to convince me that my body was disgusting. In the madrassa, our instructor had said: "But when you look at yourself in a mirror, you must notice how dirty your body is!" I'd never been able to see what they were talking about, and here in Vienna were people who devoted a whole day just to taking a handful of photos of me. They thought my body was beautiful, not unclean, and I enjoyed the attention.

I wish that someone would have told me that the pictures I was taking could be damaging to me and my future, but no one did. I would learn soon enough.

Since leaving Linz, I had avoided contact with all Pakistanis. Even going shopping in a store run by Pakistanis or Muslims, I ran the risk that they would recognize me and betray me to my father. I hid myself in plain sight: in the modeling and photography scene, where no self-respecting Muslim would find me.

When I confided in people on set about my past and told them that my parents had issued a death threat against me because I refused to marry Salman, they didn't believe me. In the first place, they couldn't believe that these kinds of things happened in Austria. And anyway, I didn't really look like someone on the run. It was difficult for others to see that I was a victim of Sharia. In their minds, a victim was weak and timid, someone who couldn't take care of herself and who hid from the world. But I was neither weak nor timid — only naive about the Western world. It would take another confrontation with the Muslim world to wake me up.

10

TAKING MY STAND

I WAS NOW nineteen years old and still homeless. In Vienna the crowd I was running with was by no means good for me, but I didn't think much about that. Survival was on my mind: the next place to sleep, the next meal to eat.

When I told the people I met at photo shoots about Jesus and the Evangelical church that I used to attend, they would laugh hard. After all, *they* were Catholics — or at least had been baptized Catholics. But, I thought, why do these Catholics not engage when I speak about Jesus? Maybe it's a Catholic thing. I didn't know all the differences between the denominations and even though I felt drawn towards the Catholic Church, its members and its clergy had no interest in helping. It would have been great to have wisdom and instruction, but when you convert, theology is not automatically "infused" into your soul to guide you. Jesus wounded my heart with love when He met me and, like Mary Magdalene, I wanted to follow Him everywhere. But now it seemed that, like Mary Magdalene, I was looking for Him like at His tomb, but without an angel telling me where to find Him.

I figured Baumann's constant drinking and partying, the endless rotation of beautiful women around him, was simply how Western people did things. I lived with drug addicts, wild party models, and men who wanted to take advantage of me. I took bad counsel from people just as broken as I was. I suppose I learned about life through my mistakes.

Even still, I had boundaries. I wouldn't snort cocaine, for instance. And, while I was comfortable posing for provocative pictures, I always asked for the negatives when I inevitably didn't want them published — even a particularly steamy shoot where I posed with some swords. The old guilt nagged me: What would my father think? To be honest, this new way of life confused me. I had little experience of the Christian world, and I thought my new life was basically normal — wild parties at villas, cocaine with strangers, men taking my pictures and then taking me to dinner every night — though of course now I know better. I don't like thinking back on this time.

After several months in Vienna, I still didn't have a place of my own. Sometimes I would stay with Baumann, and other times I would knock at a church. This roaming had become a way of life. It was another way to be homeless for Jesus. At the same time I was sleeping on couches, I was invited to all sorts of posh events with the high society of Vienna. One evening I saw the former Austrian finance minister at a party. He probably thought I was just another party girl — if only he knew the truth! Outwardly, I put on a good show, but inside me everything was broken, a pile of rubble.

Around this time, I met a man who seemed to be genuinely interested in my story. Johannes was an ex-cop, a publisher, and author of several books. He was well-known in Austria for exposing a scandal that involved the police spying for certain high-ranking members of the government. Johannes was a slender man with a narrow face framed by short brown hair and dark eyes, which to me conveyed a strange wisdom. He didn't act like other men around me. He was not excessively nice or flirtatious, but instead told me directly that he simply did not believe me after I told him my story, including the falsified marriage certificate that my father had signed for me. In Austria, he assured me, there are laws to prevent such things.

But a few weeks later, Johannes sought me out and said he had something he wanted to discuss. We arranged to have dinner near the Vienna West station.

"I believe you now," he said shortly after we had ordered.

I was taken aback at how quickly and completely he seemed to have come to this conclusion, without any help from me.

"Why did you change your mind?" I asked.

"I did some research through my contacts with the police. I saw all the statements from you and the ones from your parents. I have all the documents relating to your situation, and I believe you are telling the truth. I didn't believe you initially because I couldn't fathom such a thing happening in Austria. I'm sorry, and as an apology, I would like to offer you the chance to publish a book about your experiences."

When I told my friends about the offer, they were all excited and thought I should accept. My own enthusiasm was more limited. What right did I have to write a book? I didn't feel as though I had achieved anything; I had just left everything I knew behind. And how could I write a book if I wanted to remain in hiding? It didn't feel safe.

Nevertheless, I thought it might help other girls. And maybe other people would be happy that a Muslim became a Christian. Maybe my sister would have a better future if I became her role model. I had always longed for one myself: someone I could look up to, someone who had taken this step to freedom and succeeded. All the Pakistani girls I'd known who had rebelled had done so in secret. None of them had taken the risks I had. Occasionally there were stories about forced marriage on the news, and members of Islamic communities would be invited on talk shows. They would always claim that these were just isolated incidents and that they didn't happen in Austria. And everyone believed that the government could and would protect against it if it ever did. That was exactly what Johannes had claimed when he first met me — until he realized that, even under Austrian law, girls can be legally forced into marriage if their parents sign the certificate and threaten them with death for choosing Jesus.

So, after some reflection, I wrote the book. It was titled *From Islam to Christianity: A Death Sentence,* and within a short time it made the

Austrian bestseller list. It received national media attention because, as Johannes had predicted, nobody could believe that such a thing had taken place in Austria. Naturally, some of the people who appeared in the book went to the media. They claimed that everything in my book was false, even my faith. They said that I had made everything up to get attention and advance my career.

Shortly thereafter, the tabloid press got its hands on my privately owned modeling photos. What followed was an experience that felt uncannily familiar to what I'd gone through in Pakistan, though on the surface it looked very different. While the Muslim world wanted to shame me by covering me up, the secular world sought to shame me by revealing me undressed. A particularly scummy paper even printed the sword photos. It turned out I didn't have the only copy of the negatives — they were stolen from me by one of my "easy friends" whose house I stayed at while in Vienna. They put one of the erotic photos on one page and on the other page a photo of me praying in church. The headline read, "Sabatina James: Sharp as a Sword and as Sinful as Mary Magdalene." I was devastated. I never expected to be betrayed by so many people who had appeared to be kind to me.

To make matters even worse, my parents came forward and gave interviews to the press. They appeared on the most-watched popular TV show, where they vehemently claimed that my story was totally false. They bolstered their credibility by hiring a prestigious lawyer, a supposed defender of immigrants' rights. I knew who he was, as he had a reputation for helping refugees gain asylum — and he helped Salman. Yet here he was coming to the defense of those who were the actual perpetrators. To him, I was just a rebellious young girl who wanted to get back at her parents while getting famous.

With his help, my parents tried to stop me from telling my story by suing me for defamation. He claimed that as I had made serious allegations against my parents, I would have to prove my claims in court. Suddenly, I was being accused of being a liar who had sold out her parents and their religion because I was greedy and fame-hungry. There were moments when I hated my father. After everything he had done to me, I wished I had never been born into this family.

At the same time, I wished for a scenario in which he might apologize. I wanted to hear him say that he was sorry he didn't believe me, that he didn't realize Salman had treated me so badly in Pakistan, that he was heartbroken at what I had gone through. But he only turned against me yet again. My father claimed that I had fallen in love with Salman, but when I came back from Pakistan, I got together with another man. He wanted to forbid me from making my story and my life public. As always, his only concern was saving our family honor and preserving the reputation of Islam. My father, who had seen all his sisters marry men chosen by the family, could not understand that a woman would want to choose her own husband and her own faith. Even his own marriage had been arranged, but now my father insisted that that was not true. He said it was an ancient custom that never happened in modern times. But I knew all too well that it did — and does.

I was fuming. This was Pakistan today! Islam today! I knew that he hadn't told his relatives in Pakistan that I had converted to Christianity. For him it was a burden to have a daughter like me. Many of his friends had broken off contact. He came from a culture of shame; my father had not even seen me naked when I was a child. And now he had my book and those awful photos to prove how I had brought shame upon him.

He thought that I had converted to Christianity because I wanted to live a brazen and shameless life. The fact that I never sought out any of this attention, that I had never wanted anyone to see those pictures, that my new life was in tatters — these were things he still could not understand. I wanted desperately to explain everything, but I knew he wouldn't listen. His reaction to the book proved to me how much more he cared about his honor than rebuilding his relationship with his daughter.

The media, of course, couldn't get enough, and I found myself in the headlines regularly. It was almost worse than the brainwashing I'd undergone in the madrassa. I had no idea what crime I had committed to make the media hate me so much. Looking back today I know why.

In 2002, European attitudes about Islam were undergoing a massive transformation. In the latter decades of the twentieth century, when the trickle of Muslim immigrants to Europe became a torrent, the culture and faith of the new arrivals had been overlooked for many reasons. Austria, like all other European countries, was becoming increasingly secular: Schools had become the churches of atheists where European history, and Christianity in particular, were demeaned. It was regarded as the religion of the Inquisition, while Islam, with all its faults, was treated with kid gloves. Historical criticism was only applied to the Bible, not to the Koran. Everyone knew what could happen if anyone questioned Muhammed's rules: embassies could burn, critics could be forced to live in hiding, Muslim terrorists could fly planes into buildings, just as the world had just witnessed on September 11, 2001.

Those who criticized Islam were called "Islamophobic" or, in the most egregious cases, executed for speaking out. Meanwhile, civic leaders and the church stood idly by, and to save themselves supported false narratives about a moderate Islam. A cowardly generation attempted to appease the hungry beast, hoping it would devour them last. Of course it didn't work, and the effects of this attitude are now becoming visible all over Europe. If you teach a generation that everything the West stands for — including its religion and history — is bad, while sparing Islam from scrutiny, the lesson that this generation will learn is that the only thing sacred is Islam.

11

The Trial

Beginning around the end of the last century, Christian churches
reached out to the new Muslim arrivals to Europe in a spirit of bland
ecumenism, not understanding that their overtures were met with
contempt. In a gesture of goodwill toward Muslims, Pope St. John
Paul II famously kissed the Koran — despite the fact that the Koran
denies the death of Jesus Christ on the Cross (sura 4:157), calls Christians unbelievers destined for Hell, and refers to them as the "worst of
creatures" (sura 98:6).

Some say the pope didn't know what he was doing. But this is
far from the case. John Paul II, along with many other mid-century
Christian leaders, had a misguided and culturally detrimental understanding of Islam. Later in his life, the sainted pope during a March
2000 pilgrimage visited Wadi Al-Kharrar, where John baptized Jesus,
and declared, "May St. John the Baptist protect Islam." John Paul II
even went as far as repenting — apologizing — for the errors of the
Church over the last two thousand years.

In like manner, Mother Teresa once famously said, "I've always
said that we should help a Hindu become a good Hindu, a Muslim
become a better Muslim, a Catholic become a better Catholic." With
statements such as these, what's the point of converting?

In the age of dialogue between religions, Catholics were — and still
are — encouraged to participate in interreligious prayer gatherings. This
too was an innovation introduced by John Paul II, most famously in

the Assisi meetings, where people from different world religions came together to pray for "peace." These prayer meetings inevitably led to false understandings of prayer's efficacy and to a blurring of the difference between the supernatural faith unique to Christianity and all other faiths. Many non-Catholics drew the conclusion that religious content does not really matter, since everyone is presumably facing God. Contrary to John Paul II's intentions, the Church's openness to other faiths led to religious indifference and the dissolution of faith for many. Indeed, these interreligious gatherings are often pointed to as typical examples of the moral relativism run rampant in the Western world.

These and other similar public gestures were not without their consequences. In addition to religious indifference, they also produced guilt and shame among Christians for their past. Worse, they bolstered the Muslim belief that their religion is superior to Christianity. It's no surprise that there are hardly any conversions to Catholicism from Islam, when the leaders of the Church discourage it. That Mother Teresa and John Paul II are saints does not mean that they were right on Islam. In fact, they were wrong, terribly and dangerously wrong. Believing their message, people naively assumed that Islam was just a more exotic form of Christianity. They developed a false empathy and welcomed more and more Muslim immigration. Many bishops and religious started teaching that all religions were a way to God. They should have first informed themselves on what Islam really teaches about apostasy, about women, and about Christ. Instead, they believed that Islam could be mapped neatly onto the Christian world without the disruption that conversion stirs up.

And, in fact, I experienced this naive apathy many times as I wandered first through Linz and then Vienna. In Linz, I stopped a religious sister on the bicycle and told her that I was Christian too and that I had left Islam behind. "All religions are a way to God!" she declared. "We just have to firmly believe!" These experiences were in fact a large part of the reason why I remained Evangelical in those early days.

But after I wrote the book, all of this — the unacknowledged tensions between Islam and Christianity just beneath the surface of European life — came bursting to the surface. I was a living example of the problems with Islam, mass immigration, and the new reality in Europe. It was an uncomfortable message that rattled the media and, rather than engage, they chose to pillory me — to treat me as Islamophobic. The word *Islamophobia* was manufactured by the Muslim brotherhood in the United States to silence anyone in the West who dared question Islam. The word itself is self-contradictory. Phobias are irrational fears. But fearing a religion that demands my death sentence for apostasy was completely rational.

The press, on the other hand, was more concerned about "offending" Muslim sensitivities than it was about my potential execution for leaving Islam. In general, media figures had the desire to be seen as nice toward immigrants, without knowing much about the immigrant's religion — except that one should never criticize it. To criticize it could be dangerous: Just ask Salman Rushdie.

I was slandered and treated with sexist derision. My Christian faith was mocked and the attitude toward an Islam that demanded my death sentence was completely uncritical, almost slavish. I thought the Church would be the last place to completely fall for Islam, but most Catholics chose to be understanding multiculturalists. None of the cardinals or bishops supported me. They all remained silent — they had made their peace with Islam — while I was attacked by the press and persecuted by my family. Muslim organizations and ambassadors of Islam called me a liar online and spread lies to destroy my reputation and portray a peaceful image of Islam. They could say whatever they pleased about Islam and Muhammed: Most Westerners in their ignorance would believe them, because most Westerners had never even read a single sentence of the Koran.

One priest, Fr. Rudolph Schermann, didn't care about any of that. He was a Hungarian Catholic who was born in Turkey and had a good understanding of Muslim culture. When I told him about my experiences in the Church, he offered to baptize me. Unfortunately, he didn't tell me I needed to be confirmed. He was a kind man, but not very orthodox. He encouraged me to continue to attend Evangelical services even after I became Catholic. Yet I was just happy that a Catholic priest had finally offered to help me. And I came to trust him because he was the only one willing to be public about it. Besides, I needed all the help I could get. The Muslim community throughout the entire country had united against me: I had dishonored their religion, and I needed to be destroyed.

The journalists who tried to treat me fairly were accused of being Islamophobic and silenced. Some of them gave up writing about the issues I addressed in the book. An editor from a liberal magazine, who had once shared my story to highlight the issue of women's oppression in Islam, later confided in me, saying, "I went to the office, and suddenly I was accused of Islamophobia." Since then, she hasn't written a single critical piece. To continue would have cost her and others their careers or, worse, their heads. Still, most of the general public supported the book. They knew that tensions with Europe's fastest-growing minority were increasing rapidly, not just in Austria but everywhere else too.

As the media scrutiny worsened and the pressure from my parents grew more intense, I decided that I would remain silent in the face of all the charges leveled against me. I had additional problems of my own: I had constant suicidal thoughts and my bulimia reached its worst stage. I vomited up my life because I hated it. I hated having been born a woman, let alone a Muslim woman.

Eventually, the stress became so bad that I developed alopecia areata. Bald patches showed up on my head and I started to suffer from panic attacks in which I was short of breath and my heart pounded uncontrollably. I called a bulimia hotline. A doctor with a warm, maternal voice answered. I told her I was suffocating and that I was afraid I was going to die.

"How long have you been making yourself throw up?" she asked.

"For a while." I told her about how it had really begun in Pakistan, after Salman began abusing me and my mother beat me at home.

"You must come to the clinic immediately," she said. "This has been going on far too long."

"No, I can't come," I replied. "I'm afraid that the journalists will follow me. When they learn that I have bulimia, it'll be front-page news."

A number of other photos of me hit the tabloids soon after, and I had no idea how they landed there. I felt persecuted from all sides.

It was a terrible time. I wanted to die and feared death at the same time. I fantasized about killing myself. I wanted it to be painless. I even researched what kind of drugs I could get in a pharmacy to do it, but when I went to buy them I didn't go through with it. Jesus would not want me to end my life in this way. I tried to look for solutions instead.

Eventually I did go to the doctor. She suggested full-time therapy. But I couldn't do that — not with my court date so near. If my parents discovered I was in a hospital, they would claim that I was mentally ill and I would lose my credibility. So I did something highly unorthodox. I told the doctor that I believed in Jesus and that He would heal me. And He did. Now, when I went to throw up, I started to hear an interior voice. *You gave up your family for me. Can you give up bulimia?* I had my doubts whether this was the voice of God, but my desire to please God helped to overcome bulimia. It took at least a year, but slowly I was able to resist — without therapy but through faith.[5]

The trial began in 2004, and it seemed like an impossible battle. The first person I saw when I walked into the courtroom was my mother. She was there, sitting across from me, and I thought back to my earliest memories of her cooking in our kitchen in Pakistan. I could smell the spices simmering on the stove. I thought of all the things I'd promised

---

[5] I am not suggesting that others should do the same. Bulimia has many causes. Mine went back to abuse, and when I started to replace bad memories — especially of the sexual abuse by my cousin — with the words that God says about me, I was able to overcome it.

my father as a child: how I would make him proud and be an honorable daughter to him. The only thing I wanted in that moment was to go to my father and massage his feet, to show him how much I loved him.

Now I was sitting across from them in a courtroom, unsure of how we'd reached this point. I was terrified my father would end up in prison because of me. I couldn't believe I'd done this to him. My father had the same look on his face as he had during our meeting at the homeless shelter years before. It was a look that said, "What have you done to me? I have brought you to Austria, I have given you a new life, and because of you I have lost everything."

I felt all the guilt that Islam had bred in me and all the hopelessness that the trial had instilled. I was begging for help and protection from the Austrian authorities, and I feared they wouldn't give it to me. I thought I would lose the trial, that I would be ostracized by Christians and Muslims alike.

In that moment I wanted to go back to my family. I wanted to take back everything I'd said and done. If I go back, I thought, at least I'll have something. At least I won't be alone.

It was painful enough to be defending myself against my own family, but I was being asked to prove things that were nearly impossible to prove: How do you prove that you were married involuntarily when the Austrian embassy validated the marriage certificate? How do you prove that your mother beat you six years previously, or that your cousin sexually abused you in another country? I was being asked to prove everything I had been through while also being forced to relive it. All the harassment and threats I had lived with since running away were now being played out in the public sphere.

To make matters worse, many of the people I thought I could depend on during this time disappeared. It was too dangerous for them politically. Supporting me would mean being critical of Islam, and they would appear culturally insensitive. They did not want to face the anger of the Muslim community as I had done. Many of my so-called friends disappeared during this time too. Many of my supposed "friends" had sold me out to the tabloids. Everyone feared what my father and the Pakistani community might do. And while my social workers from the homeless shelter came to the trial, they didn't testify either. When I asked them why, they told me that they were afraid of my father's reaction and said they'd given all their information in writing to the judge. I was glad that they had done that, and of all people they were the most supportive. They just couldn't make statements on my behalf in an open courtroom, because it would put the shelter and everyone who went there in danger.

Their fears were not unfounded. One of my former teachers had been asked to testify. My father went to her house, just standing outside, staring and waiting. He also went to see Frieda in Sarleinsbach and told her she had to testify that everything I'd written was a lie. She said she couldn't, because as far as she could tell, it was the truth, and all the things I wrote about Sarleinsbach were exactly as she remembered them. My father didn't threaten anyone physically in the way he threatened me, but he got his message across.

There were only a few people left whom I could count on to testify on my behalf. And it was the court that decided who would be called to make a statement.

One of them was my best friend from the high achievers' school in Linz. She came to court with her father and was shaking with fear as she approached the stand. When the judge asked her father to let her speak by herself, he refused to leave her side. He said he knew my father and was afraid that he would harm his daughter if he left her alone.

Tarek also testified. We had broken up and we weren't in touch any longer, but it was perhaps his testimony and the written information of the counselors from the homeless shelter that most swayed the court. Tarek had nothing to gain by supporting my word against my parents, but he told the judge how terrified I'd been in the months after leaving home, how my father had threatened to kill me for becoming a

Christian, how violent and angry the Pakistani community had been toward me. His statements and the written information of the counselors from the homeless shelter painted a sympathetic picture for the court and counteracted some of the damage the tabloids had done.

My family, on the other hand, made a persuasive case to discredit me. When the judge questioned my brothers, who look completely Western, they answered that there had never been any problems at home. My mother had never hit me, they said, and I had been overjoyed at the prospect of marrying Salman. Our Austrian neighbors testified that my father was well-adjusted, moderate in his beliefs, and would never hurt me. All of my family's friends went on the record to say that the marriage between Salman and me had been mutual and that nobody had ever threatened to kill me or hurt me in any way. It was the same performance my parents had given to the social workers years before, but on a much larger scale.

I prayed that the judge would see the truth behind these fabrications. Before the trial began a friend had recited the words of Christ from the Gospel of Luke to me: "When you are brought before synagogues, rulers and authorities, do not worry about how you will defend yourselves or what you will say, for the Holy Spirit will teach you at that time what you should say" (Luke 12:11–12).

In the end, what saved me was the performance itself. When probed, my brothers' stories that there had never been any problems in the home had holes in them. They admitted that they weren't often home after school and so couldn't have known whether my mother beat me or not. When my mother was called to testify, the judge began asking her tough questions about our relationship. She was not prepared for such intense questioning, and she eventually lost track of her story. When she was asked what had happened when they left me in Pakistan, my mother blurted out, "Well she brought so much shame on the family! I was glad she was gone so I didn't have to look at her."

Finally, my father admitted that he had signed the marriage certificate in my name. He claimed he was allowed to do this as my legal guardian, but it was enough to contradict his claim that I'd married Salman voluntarily. My parents simply couldn't understand why I had brought so much "shame" on them for the sake of Christianity, which they could never take seriously. They thought that my refusal to marry, my conversion, and now the publishing of the book was my way of hurting them or an obscene bid at fame. They truly believed that I was brainwashed by evil people and had some sort of mental disorder. Muslims refuse to understand why anyone would leave Islam for Christianity — people convert to Islam, not the other way around!

I will never forget Abba's face when he looked at me. His eyes, always eager to see me when he came back to Pakistan from Austria, now welled with tears. He felt betrayed. And he didn't understand what he had done wrong. And my mother cried beside him and opened her arms. "Please come back!" Her words tore through me, but I also knew what they meant. *Embrace Islam! Choose us over Christ.* My heart pounded within me. I was shaking but tried to remain strong. Had I known then that this was the last time I would see my parents, I would have fainted.

When the judge announced the verdict, I was a wreck. Hardly anyone had supported me, and many of the people whom I'd thought I could trust had sided with my parents and testified against me. But I was acquitted. The court judged my words to be "authentic and accurate" and ruled that I had not defamed my family. It also found that tabloid pictures had been printed in violation of my privacy. I began to sob. I no longer had to defend myself against my family's accusations, but I still didn't feel like I was free. I had lost as much as I'd won.

The effects of that day live within me even now. People tell me that my mother doesn't smile anymore. They say my conversion is the cause of her suffering. And Abba is treated like an outcast within the Muslim community. A woman whom I had known since my childhood sent me an email saying: "Your parents arrived in Pakistan. No one spoke to them. You have extinguished your father's pride. You have taken his honor." Those words hurt me, but I know in my heart that my life then and my life now is not about me or my parents; it is about Christ.

> *Dear Mother,*
>
> *Can you feel it when I cry? I wish I would have brought joy into your life, but instead you are condemned to weep for the rest of your life. Sometimes I wish I could lay my arms around you to console you, but this is only a dream. Daughters have many dreams that they want to come true. My dream is to give you a hug. And recently God did me a favor. I was at our house standing outside. You came out. I embraced you and ran away.*
>
> *Is there a daughter who is so afraid of her mother? Is there a child who is afraid to die at the hands of the woman who nursed her? Why does it have to be like this? I love you, Mother. Forever will I love you and forever will I weep over losing you. This is the peace that Christ gave me for preferring Him over you, dear mother. My peace consists in mourning and shedding tears for losing you and Abba and Aisha, Adnan and Manzoor. You are my sacrificial offering to Christ. Like Abraham did with Isaac, so I bring you to the altar. This must be the blessedness that Jesus means, to prefer tears of sacrifice to the joys a family can give. Now will I mourn for your loss and the many persecutions of my enemies, and one day I shall be comforted by seeing the Holy Face of Jesus. This is my hope.*

12

Returning to Pakistan

With the publication of my book and the trial that followed, I found myself thrust into an unexpected spotlight. But this was a different kind of attention — one that reached across borders, filling my inbox and mailbox with letters from strangers. From every corner of Europe and beyond, messages poured in.

The book had struck a nerve, particularly in Germany, where its words resonated deeply. Muslim girls, converts to Christianity, and countless others who had lived similar struggles wrote to me, their voices echoing my own. They thanked me for speaking aloud the truths they had been forced to whisper. Their gratitude was moving, but beneath it lay a frustration I hadn't anticipated. I had always known there were others like me, but I had never grasped the sheer scale of it — the silent suffering, the unseen battles being fought in homes and hearts.

I wanted to help. I needed to. But how?

Friends offered suggestions. Some urged me toward show business — acting, singing, the dreams of my youth — arguing that fame could be a powerful tool, a megaphone for the causes I now carried. The idea tempted me, but I hesitated. Was that the path forward? Or was there another way to turn my voice into something truly unstoppable?

Then, one evening on the tram, a woman caught my eye. At first, I thought she was simply staring, but then she stepped closer, her expression a mix of recognition and urgency.

"I know you," she said. "I saw you on TV."

There was no small talk, no polite hesitation. Instead, she leaned in, lowering her voice as if afraid someone might overhear. "Someone I know — someone very close to me — is about to be forced into marriage. I don't know what to do. Can you help?"

Her words hit me like a gust of wind, scattering the doubts I had been wrestling with. This wasn't just about letters or distant voices on a page — this was real, immediate, and happening right in front of me.

I wanted to answer her, to promise I'd do something, but the truth was I had no idea where to begin. So I did the only thing I knew how to do. I turned to God in prayer and, as always, to the Bible. Somewhere in its pages, I hoped, I would find the guidance I so desperately needed.

In Paul's letter to Timothy, he says, "All scripture, inspired of God, is profitable to teach, to reprove, to correct, to instruct in justice, That the man of God may be perfect, furnished to every good work" (2 Tim. 3:16–17, DRA).

The good work I was supposed to do became quite clear to me after opening the book of the prophet Isaiah to the following verses: "I, the Lord, have called you in righteousness; I will take hold of your hand. I will keep you and will make you to be a covenant for the people and a light for the Gentiles, to open eyes that are blind, to free captives from prison and to release from the dungeon those who sit in darkness" (42:6–7).

A revelation settled over me, undeniable and urgent — I was here for a purpose. I was meant to set the captives free, to open the eyes of the blind, to expose the truth about the growing threat of Islam to the West. Too many refused to see it, too many chose silence over confrontation. But I could not.

In 2006, driven by the words of the prophet Isaiah and joined by a group of like-minded individuals, I took action. Together, we launched an organization dedicated to rescuing victims of forced marriage and freeing Christians from oppression. This was not just a cause; it was a calling. A battle for those who had no voice. And I was ready to fight.

With the help of my Evangelical friends, I had escaped Austria, seeking refuge in Germany from the growing hostility of the Muslim community. I had hoped for safety, a fresh start. But danger has a way of following close behind.

Before long, my family uncovered my location. Their reach extended farther than I had imagined, and soon, I found myself at risk once more. The German police stepped in, placing me under victim protection. A police protection officer was assigned to me, guiding me in regard to my safety. For two years, I lived with my Evangelical friends, who never asked for rent or repayment. To them, my mission to help others was a divine calling, and they believed supporting me was theirs.

After my book was released in Germany, doors began to open. I was invited onto major television programs, asked to give lectures, and suddenly found myself in direct contact with others who had suffered under the weight of so-called "honor violence." One of them was Hanife Gashi.

Her grief was immeasurable. Her daughter, only sixteen, had been murdered by her own father — a man who believed she had strayed too far from tradition, embracing a life he saw as a disgrace. What began in Kosovo with a forced marriage ended in Germany with a senseless killing. Convinced that his child had tarnished the family's honor simply because she had a boyfriend, he ended her life and discarded her body in a lake.

Hanife spoke of her loss with quiet, aching strength. I listened, horrified yet unsurprised. These tragedies were far too common, buried in silence, suffered behind closed doors. And at that moment, I knew I could never look away.

Then there was Rehana, a convert from Islam to Christianity. A Protestant pastor had taken care of her, but the authorities wanted to send her back to Afghanistan where she was born. Rehana was just a child when she was forced into marriage at thirteen. Barely more than a girl herself, she soon became a mother, her youth stolen before she had a chance to live it. Yet despite the hardship, she possessed a beauty that was almost unreal — delicate features and deep, large, sorrowful eyes that held the weight of a life she had never chosen.

She fled Afghanistan after the Taliban gunned down her parents, seeking safety in Germany, clinging to the hope of a future free from fear. With the help of Protestant missionaries, she embraced Christianity, a decision that would mark her forever.

When I met her, she was trembling, tears streaking her face. She lifted her sleeve to point to her arm. "My husband did this," she whispered. He had struck her for daring to remove her headscarf, for claiming even the smallest piece of freedom.

But that was only part of her suffering. She was destitute, struggling to raise two children alone, trapped between an abusive home and an uncertain future. Fear consumed her — not just of the man who hurt her, but of something even greater. If she were deported back to Afghanistan, there would be no second chance. Apostasy meant death.

Her voice shook as she spoke, desperation threading every word. She was running out of time, and she knew it.

I sat beside Rehana as she faced her first interview with the German authorities. The man across the desk regarded her with cool detachment, his voice clipped, his skepticism thinly veiled. He pressed her about her conversion, but when she hesitated over details of Christian feast days, his doubt hardened into something unmovable.

Rehana blinked, bewildered. Feast days? She knew nothing of them. She only knew Jesus. And in her quiet, earnest way, she spoke of Him — not as a scholar, but as someone whose heart had been transformed.

It wasn't enough. In the end, her asylum request was denied. I refused to accept it.

At one of my lectures, a lawyer had approached me, offering free legal aid for those in need. I turned to him now, and together, we fought. For months, he battled the system, challenging the rejection at every turn. And finally, justice prevailed. Rehana was granted the right to stay, free to build a life in Germany with her children.

That victory lit a fire in me. If I could help her, how many more could I save?

For the next three years, I fought relentlessly, advocating for women trapped in the same cycle of fear and oppression. Each case reinforced my purpose, each triumph fueled my resolve. I believed I had found my mission.

But then something disrupted my peace.

The past crept back, whispering in the edges of my mind. Memories of Faiza — the woman from my childhood, battered and broken — began to haunt me. It was as if her voice was calling from across time and distance, urging me toward a place where suffering was even greater.

Pakistan.

And I knew I had to answer.

In 2008, Pakistan and Afghanistan were ranked among the most dangerous places on earth. Returning as a convert would be more than just reckless — it would be a death sentence.

If discovered, I would face one of two fates. A religious mob, frenzied by a sense of divine justice, would tear me apart in the streets — just as they had done to countless others before me. Or, if I was formally charged with blasphemy, the government itself would seal my fate. A conviction would mean either execution or a lifetime behind bars, where death row was its own kind of hell — abuse, rape, torture, a slow descent into madness.

I knew all of this. And yet something inside me still whispered, *Go.*

For months, I wrestled with the thought, paralyzed by fear. How could I take such a risk? Was this truly the will of God? If I could be certain of that, I would go — even if terror clung to me like a shadow.

At the time, I was still attending an Evangelical church, a place that had become more than just a place of worship — it was my community. Whenever I needed to flee, whether from my own family or the enraged families of those I had helped, the doors of the church were always open. My list of enemies grew daily, but the Evangelicals never wavered. They sheltered me without hesitation, without ever asking for anything in return.

One friend once told me, "I am most thankful to God that someone persecuted for Christ's sake is living under my roof." I had never heard love expressed so purely. Not even in the Catholic community I am now a part of.

As I wrestled with the terrifying prospect of returning to Pakistan, fate — or perhaps divine intervention — brought Richard into my life.

He was a German missionary, one of the few who had traveled to Pakistan multiple times, an anomaly in a place where foreigners were either feared or watched. Most mistook him for a tourist, allowing him to move freely without suspicion. He had seen the country's darkness up close, yet he wasn't afraid. And to my astonishment, he encouraged me to go with him.

But was this truly God's will?

The question consumed me. I searched my heart, yet all I found was fear. I needed certainty, something undeniable that would tell me whether this path had been laid before me by God Himself — or I was simply walking toward my own destruction.

So I turned to the Bible.

My fingers trembled as I flipped through its pages, searching for an answer. Then, in the book of Joshua, I found these words: "Be strong and steadfast! Do not fear nor be dismayed, for the Lord, your God, is with you wherever you go" (1:9, NABRE). I closed the Bible, exhaling slowly.

"I'm going to Pakistan."

The words felt both terrifying and liberating.

My fear was immense, an ever-present weight pressing against my ribs. But I could not ignore the words of God. It is one thing to read them, to let them roll off the tongue in moments of comfort, and another to live them. It is effortless to imagine oneself brave when courage is merely an abstract virtue, a distant ideal requiring no immediate action. But true courage? True courage is something else entirely.

It is the courage of prophets who spoke truth with death at their doorstep. The courage of saints who stood unwavering as the world scorned them. It is the courage to stare into the impossible and step forward regardless, knowing that only God can make such a thing bearable.

Did I possess that courage?

If the moment came — if a jihadi stood before me, his hatred burning hotter than his weapon — would I stand my ground? Could I meet him as Joshua met the giants, as David faced Goliath? Not with the assurance of safety, but with the unshakable conviction that God's will must be done?

Yes. If He required it of me, then yes.

My life was no longer mine to keep. I had already surrendered everything to Him — why should I grasp at it now? There were no promises of safety, no divine contract shielding me from harm. But I had something greater: faith. And faith whispered that this mission was not my own but His, that I was not the architect of this path but merely a servant called to walk it.

The faith of Joshua inspired me to face the giants. The first one stood before me now — my victims' protection officer.

He had once called me his "nightmare case." Now, as I sat across from him and told him I was going to Pakistan, he looked at me as if I had truly lost my mind.

"Horribly imprudent," he muttered, rubbing his temples.

He wasn't alone in thinking this. Every person I confided in tried to dissuade me. Even those who admired my cause believed I was throwing myself into reckless danger. "If anything happens to you in Pakistan, the German government would be powerless to intervene. As an Austrian citizen, you will be on your own!" the police protection officer reminded me.

But the voice of God had already settled the matter in my heart. I had left Pakistan as a Muslim, never seeing the suffering of its persecuted Christian minority. Now, I could not help them from afar. I had to know them. I had to listen to their sorrow.

And so, in 2008, I packed a few belongings and left for Pakistan with Richard, carrying nothing but faith and the desire to aid the afflicted Church. I had no money, but I prayed that God would make me capable enough, that His grace would be sufficient to bring comfort where I had nothing material to offer.

What good is a Christian if their life is not spent for others?

The Jesus I had met in the Bible was like that. The prophets too. And that was my new ummah — not one of blood and tribe, but of love and justice.

My last memories of Pakistan resurfaced as the plane descended. The last time I was there, I was a prisoner of Islam. Now, I had returned to set prisoners free. That was the transformation Jesus had brought into my life.

The heat struck us like a hammer the moment we stepped out of the airport. It was a different kind of heat than in Europe — thick, suffocating, clinging to the skin like an embrace that wouldn't let go.

Waiting for us were Asma and Saif.

Saif was a convert from Islam, a man who had survived prison, a man whose own family had once tried to poison him. He had lived, but not without consequences. His health had never fully recovered. It was only through the intervention of Evangelical advocates that he had escaped death.

Our journey began the very next morning.

I was exhausted, my body screaming for rest, but the azan shattered the early morning silence before the sun had even risen. The imam sang the call to prayer, his voice struggling through the high notes, breathless and uneven. He sounded asthmatic. My grandfather had done a much better job.

Then came another surprise.

Asma and Saif had hired a driver. A Muslim. From Peshawar.

My stomach twisted. Peshawar — the stronghold of the Pakistani Taliban. A place where al-Qaeda leaders and bin Laden's closest aides had lived and hidden.

I turned to Asma and Saif, my pulse quickening. "You hired a driver from *Peshawar*?"

Saif only smiled. "Don't worry. He thinks you're family, visiting from abroad. That's how we introduced you."

I forced myself to exhale. I had walked into the lion's den.

And the lions didn't even know I was there.

Asma's voice was calm, but her words sent a fresh chill through me.

"In the areas we're going to, we need a man as our driver. Without him, we won't make it back."

Oh, great. Not only were we in one of the most dangerous countries in the world, but we were also heading straight into its most treacherous region — with a man who might very well be a Taliban member himself.

The weight of our situation settled over me like a suffocating blanket. I wanted to believe Asma and Saif knew what they were doing, but doubt gnawed at the edges of my faith. What if we had just climbed into a car with our executioner?

We had to travel at night. The daytime heat was unbearable — over 100 degrees Fahrenheit, thick with humidity that made every breath feel like drowning. Our car was ancient, its metal frame baking in the relentless climate. No air conditioning. No seatbelts. Just the road stretching endlessly before us and the darkness pressing in from all sides.

Hours passed. The rhythmic hum of the engine and the exhaustion of the journey pulled me under, and I drifted into uneasy sleep.

Then — a sudden jolt. My eyes snapped open. Something wasn't right.

The atmosphere inside the car had changed, thick with unspoken tension. Saif and the driver were speaking in hushed voices, their words clipped and urgent. Our security guard — a man with a gun, who had been a silent presence the entire journey — remained motionless, staring straight ahead.

I strained to listen, but their words were swallowed by the night.

Then the car lurched. A sickening thud reverberated through the frame, and the vehicle jolted violently.

Saif and the driver saw it first. A body. A human corpse had been thrown directly at our car.

My stomach twisted. My pulse thundered in my ears. Before I could react, the driver slammed his foot on the gas, and the car shot forward. We were being chased.

The tires screeched against the dirt road as we swerved wildly, barely maintaining control. The driver's hands were locked on the wheel. Fear coiled around my throat like a noose. This was it. This was the end.

I barely had time to think, to process, to scream.

Instead, I prayed. I clung to the only thing I had left — the only thing that had ever sustained me.

"He hath given his angels charge over thee; to keep thee in all thy ways."

These words of the psalm of King David echoed in my mind, a whisper against the roar of terror. I held onto them as the darkness swallowed us whole.

And miraculously, God's angels did save us.

Our driver, with instincts honed by years of survival in this brutal landscape, got us out. He maneuvered the car into the safety of a populated area, where others could protect us. The murderers disappeared into the night. I had no idea why they left or why they had come after us in the first place. Would they return? The fear gnawed at me. But one thing was now certain: If I had to travel in Pakistan again, I would trust no one but a Muslim man from Peshawar to drive me.

Not long after, another battle began — one I couldn't outrun.

Sickness.

I had been surviving on bananas, my only safe option amid the filth of the so-called "restaurants" that lined our route. Sanitation was nonexistent. But suddenly, my stomach twisted in pain, a fever surged through my body, and waves of nausea overtook me. By the time we arrived at the hotel — if it could even be called that — I was barely standing. The room was a nightmare. The shower and bed crawled with creatures, some familiar, others unidentifiable. When I complained, the hotel manager casually sprayed the place. Within seconds, the infestation was dead.

I stared at the room, now filled with the acrid stench of chemicals and the carcasses of insects. And I was supposed to sleep here? Sick, feverish, surrounded by poisoned bodies?

My condition worsened, and I was taken to a local clinic. The doctor recommended an infusion, but when I saw the state of the facility — the grime, the haphazard handling of used needles — I refused. Better to endure the illness than risk something far worse.

"The victims are waiting," I reminded myself. Resting now would mean failing them. So, I took a bucket for my sickness and pressed on.

At our next stop, men with weapons guarded the entrance of our so-called hotel. I was told to keep silent. Not that I could have spoken — I was too weak to utter a word.

Then the news came. One of the victims who had been coming to meet me had been shot.

Fear gripped me. Was it too dangerous to continue? Should we turn back?

Saif's words cut through my doubt.

"Remember Queen Esther," he said. "She risked her life to save her people."

I swallowed hard. He was right. I whispered a prayer and gathered what little strength remained in me. And I went.

And oh, what a beautiful day it was.

The moment we arrived, I was met by a sea of faces — women, children, even elderly men who had come to support them. Some began to sing. Rose petals were scattered at my feet. Garlands of flowers were draped around my neck. Babies, naked and without diapers, were placed in my arms.

I had no strength left, but it didn't matter.

Love is not in grand gestures — it is in presence, in showing up even in weakness. At that moment, the words of the apostles came alive within me: "For Christ's sake, I delight in weaknesses, in insults, in hardships, in persecutions, in difficulties. For when I am weak, then I am strong" (2 Cor. 12:10).

It was never me doing this work. It was God. It had always been God.

I met women who had been raped. Christians who had been persecuted. Slaves — because yes, in Pakistan, slavery still exists.

Most of these slaves are Christians, trapped in the homes of wealthy Muslim families or forced to toil in brick kilns. Many are never allowed to receive the sacraments, never permitted to set foot in a church. Their day begins before dawn and ends long after dusk. When they fall ill, no doctor comes. A cough or cancer — it makes no difference. A sick child is left to die alone. And if any of them dares to complain, they are beaten or, worse, accused of blasphemy.

I heard the story of Meera and Iqbal. They had children. Meera was pregnant when they burned her alive — thrown into the same kiln where the bricks were made. And no one cared.

The life of a Christian, here, was worth less than the dirt beneath one's feet.

From Sindh, I traveled to see a woman named Sohaila. Her son had been murdered, condemned for a crime he did not commit.

Before I could enter her home, I had to leap from stone to stone, avoiding the canal water that had collected in front of her building. We sat on the roof to speak — away from the countless children who had swarmed me upon my arrival. Sohaila didn't want them to hear how their brother was murdered. She was on her own. Sohaila's story was one of unbearable loss.

Her husband, unable to withstand the grief of their son's unjust execution, suffered a heart attack and died. Now she was alone, left with her underage children — children who should have been in school, playing, dreaming. Instead, they dragged a cart of vegetables through the streets, struggling to earn enough to keep their mother and siblings alive.

She had done everything to save her son. She had knocked on every door: human rights organizations, the church, anyone who might listen. She had prayed, pleaded, and wept. But the world had turned its back on her. Her son had been sentenced to death, and no one — not the law, not society, not even the institutions meant to protect the innocent — had come to his defense.

In this land, there was only one escape from captivity. Only one way to avoid execution, imprisonment, or the wrath of the mob.

Conversion. Deny Christ, and you might live. Refuse, and you will suffer the fate of Sohaila's son.

The poor mother's eyes were reddened and drowning in tears when she held the picture of her son like a relic in her hands. They had taken off his clothes, beaten him, and abused him. And he sat there in his prison cell when she saw him. "Be quick!" he had told her. "They have plans to kill me." No one helped or could help. Sohaila's son was hanged. Sohaila no longer had any joy, and it was astonishing how she was able to cope in raising her other children.

Sometimes, when I speak to people in the West about the sufferings of martyrs, they remind me that while the Church in Pakistan endures unimaginable horrors, Christians in the West face their own struggles — the burdens of ordinary life. I hear this often in the United States, where many are so consumed by the discomforts of daily existence that they fail to grasp the true weight of persecution. It infuriates me when trivial inconveniences are spoken of as if they are insurmountable trials.

People like Sohaila are not spared the tribulations of ordinary life simply because they endure persecution. Her husband is dead, and in the depths of her grief, she must still manage the daily struggles of raising a large family. In Pakistan, the average Christian household has eight children, most of whom will never set foot in a school. Education is a luxury afforded only to the wealthy. And even when a Christian family manages to scrape together enough to send their children to school, they are forced to study the Koran. If those children happen to be girls, fear is ever-present: Will they return home? Each year, more than a thousand Christian girls vanish, their fates sealed in whispered transactions. Some are forced into conversion, others sold to gangs, their innocence bartered like trinkets in a soulless marketplace.

I wanted to hear their stories, to hold their truths in my hands like fragile, shattered glass. But just as I was about to visit someone in prison who needed help, my contacts, Saif and Saima, turned the warning inward. "The one who needs help right now is you," they told me. A hostile Islamic group had taken notice of my presence. Every meeting had to be canceled — both for my safety and for the protection of the victims. After days of bearing witness to the persecuted, I was confined to Saima's house. And then, within days, I had to flee Pakistan altogether. Later, I learned that had I remained just a little longer, I would have probably shared the fate of those I sought to help: imprisoned, silenced, forgotten.

After my return, I dedicated myself to aiding persecuted Christians in Pakistan and victims of forced marriage in Germany. Some of the girls I encountered there had been married off at just fourteen. In the eyes of many, there was nothing unusual about this — after all, the Prophet himself had wed a young girl. The violence these child brides endured was beyond comprehension. They were beaten with belts, burned with irons, their cries dismissed as the shrill complaints of disobedient women. One girl we helped in Hamburg, Germany, was partially deaf, her husband's fury having slammed her skull against a wall until the world rang in hollow silence. Now, she and others like her fled, clutching infants still in diapers, their futures dissolving into uncertainty.

We hid them, moving them from place to place across Germany. But time and again, they were found. It became clear that the system itself betrayed them. One girl, fleeing a forced marriage, was located by her own aunt, an employee at a prestigious German bank. By accessing confidential banking records, she pinpointed where the girl had last withdrawn money and passed the information to the family. And just like that, they found her. So much for Western privacy laws — honor, in their eyes, eclipsed all.

Other times, the hunt was more insidious. When a girl fled, her photo would be circulated in mosques, her entire community transformed into a network of watchful eyes. In one case, the father of a girl we sheltered stood outside the very house where we had hidden her, his presence a silent, unwavering threat.

But the legal system was perhaps the greatest betrayal of all. When young mothers escaped with their children, their husbands would secure high-powered lawyers, demanding custody. It didn't matter how well we hid the girls — the courts, oblivious or complicit, handed them back to their abusers. The men knew how to manipulate the system, how to wear the mask of modernity in court while maintaining a reign of terror in private. Judges were charmed. The girls, forced to face their fathers and brothers in court, trembled in fear, their voices barely above a whisper.

I stood beside one such girl, a former child bride, now older but still shackled by the past. As we entered the courtroom, her father and male relatives erupted in fury, their voices like a storm breaking over us. "Infidel! Infidel!" they spat at me, heedless of the police, the cameras, the solemn weight of the law. And yet, despite the threats, despite the evidence, the judge ruled in their favor. The girl lost her case.

She could not endure life on the run. The fear, the isolation, the endless pursuit — it became too much. And so, she returned to her family, stepping back into the abyss she had fought so desperately to escape. She deserved protection. Instead, she was devoured by the very hands that had sworn to keep her safe.

I am continually disheartened that the political left, which so ardently champions the cause of anti-racism, turns a blind eye to the silent suffering of these Muslim women. They do not suffer because they rejected Western ideals, but because they embraced them — because they dared to claim the rights that the free world takes for granted, only to find themselves abandoned when they needed protection most. The reasons for this neglect seem not accidental but deliberate. A woman who dares to critique Islam — an ideology wrapped in the armor of victimhood — becomes an inconvenient truth. Her suffering dismantles the carefully crafted illusion that all faiths are equally benign, that all cultures are equally just.

After years of aiding young women in Hamburg, I moved to Mannheim, a city in southern Germany, with nothing but a single, battered suitcase. I had grown accustomed to fleeing, to vanishing without a trace when the shadows grew too long. It wasn't long before a young Pakistani girl sought me out, her voice trembling. "They have spoken of you in the mosque," she warned. "One of them said he followed you and knows where you live."

The weight of her words settled over me like an omen. I packed my bag and left before the walls could close in.

This girl, like so many others, had found herself ensnared in a life not of her own choosing. Recognizing me in a store, she had begged for help to escape the violence of her own family. I did what I could, even daring to step inside her home, knowing the risks. But soon, Mannheim itself became inhospitable. Strangers glared at me with undisguised malice. The whispers turned to open hostility. One morning, I stepped into a bakery, only to find a Muslim woman behind the counter staring through me, as though I were a ghost. She refused to serve me. A German colleague hesitated before stepping forward. "I'm sorry," she murmured. "She won't serve you because you left Islam."

That was my final warning. Mannheim, too, was lost to me.

And so I have lived ever since — forever on the move, forever pursued, yet never afraid. My time in Pakistan altered the course of my life. Amidst the cruelty, amidst the fear, God whispered to me: "Stand before the giants and do not tremble." And so I stand unwavering, as He shields me time and again. From a single ember of faith, a great fire has risen.

In the years that followed, Friends of the Passion gave birth to Operation Moses, a mission to free Christian slaves from their chains. We have stood beside thousands of victims of unjust blasphemy laws, given refuge to converts fleeing persecution in Nigeria, and built homes for orphaned children left behind in the wreckage. Where the world remains indifferent, we act. Where others falter, we remain unshaken. "We are hard pressed on every side, but not crushed; perplexed, but not in despair; persecuted, but not abandoned; struck down, but not destroyed" (2 Cor. 4:8–12).

13

Coming Home

Fleeing Mannheim marked the beginning of an undeniable change within me, one that would shape the course of my life forever. It did not arrive with fanfare, nor like a flash of lightning. Rather, it was a slow, deliberate awakening, a whispering truth that grew louder with each passing day. I was becoming Catholic — not merely in name, but in the depth of my being. This transformation was not abrupt, nor was it crafted by the influence of the German Church. It was written by the guiding hand of Divine Providence.

At that time, I had found refuge with a welcoming Evangelical family near Stuttgart. Their hospitality was a gift from God. Their home, nestled in a small village surrounded by towering trees, vast farms, and open meadows, felt like a sanctuary. The village, with its cobbled streets and quaint half-timbered homes, seemed to be frozen in time, offering a peaceful retreat. Rolling hills stretched beyond the village, where vineyards and fields of wildflowers painted the landscape in vibrant colors. The air was fresh, and the gentle hum of nature provided a constant, soothing soundtrack. It was a place where the beauty of the countryside and the warmth of community perfectly intertwined, offering both solace and tranquility.

"For months, I prayed about whether I should rent out part of our large home," the mother told me. "But when I heard your story, I knew God wanted me to offer it to you freely. You're welcome to stay for a year — or even longer if you need."

The family had three children my age, and they believed that by sheltering a persecuted Christian, they would receive blessings in return. They were truly wonderful people — but their church, which was located in the nearby city of Stuttgart, was another story entirely.

They were part of a charismatic community, where faith was expressed through raised hands, trembling voices, and bold declarations of victory. For them, belief was a triumphant path, and blessings served as evidence of God's favor. I marveled at their devotion, yet something felt amiss.

One day, for instance, I asked a prayer leader to intercede for a Christian woman languishing on death row in Pakistan. "We sit here on cozy benches, while she sits in prison for our faith," I remarked. My words, though sincere, were met with an uneasy stillness. My fellow Christians did not deny that suffering existed; they just placed more emphasis on the miracles of Jesus. It seemed to me that by speaking about the woman on death row they felt as if I were challenging them to drink from the chalice of the Passion — something that they would rather not do.

In that vast congregation, where the Spirit was said to move with power, I felt only the emptiness of absence. I wondered if I was unworthy of blessing — if my life, marked by persecution and devoid of abundance, had made me less than them. All I had was a suitcase, carried from place to place, with no victory to claim, no blessings to show.

I recall one night in particular. As the music blared, the voices rose, and my heart, instead of swelling with joy, could hardly bear it. Everyone around me was "filled with the Holy Spirit," but all I felt was affliction — the scars of losses endured for the very faith that seemed to have granted them abundance. As I ran out of the congregation hall, one of the worshippers saw me and followed.

"What happened?" she asked, her voice tinged with concern. I looked at her and replied, "Either you are wrong, or I am wrong, but one of us is wrong."

I prayed after this conversation, and it became clear to me once again that my very afflictions were, in fact, my abundance. The gift God had given me was the constant presence of His Cross — and in that, the presence of Christ Himself. All this time, He had been with me, not in the absence of suffering, but through it.

St. Paul, when in prison, wrote in his letter to the Philippians: "For it has been granted to you that for the sake of Christ you should not only believe in him but also suffer for his sake, engaged in the same conflict which you saw and now hear to be mine" (1:29–30, RSVCE). And later: "But whatever gain I had, I counted as loss for the sake of Christ. . . . For his sake I have suffered the loss of all things, and count them as refuse, in order that I may gain Christ" (3:7–8, RSVCE).

It's true that all I had was a suitcase and no home, but now, I suddenly felt wealthier than my friends with their grand homes. I felt freer because God had granted me the grace to leave all things behind. That, I realized, was the greater gift.

And yet, there seemed to be something missing. In the Evangelical churches I knew, Christ was always spoken of, but I began to realize that He was strangely absent. The cross was there, but it was empty.

One day, pointing to the cross, I asked my pastor: "Where is Christ? Why is He not there?"

"He is risen," the pastor replied. "He is not there anymore." "But," I said to him, "He was just crucified in Syria, so He is still there, suffering in our brothers." The pastor didn't understand what I meant.

It was 2014. The jihadist group Islamic State (ISIS) had taken over parts of Syria and Iraq. They carried out public executions and tied bloodied bodies to wooden crosses to enforce the strict rules of Sharia law. Bodies of the executed were left on crosses for days as a warning.

I interviewed a Christian who had been working in Libya when ISIS arrived — one of the few who managed to escape. Sitting in my friend's dining room, he began to share his story with me. The wooden table was long, and as we sipped our chai, I could feel the warmth of the moment, even as the children ran back and forth around the house. My friend's home was always open, always welcoming, even to the littlest ones, so the lively chaos was nothing unusual. The beauty of nature surrounded us, visible through the almost transparent wall that felt like a seamless window, making it seem as though we were sitting outside, immersed in the peacefulness of the outdoors. It was a perfect setting, for the story he was about to tell me was harrowing — one that would leave a lasting mark on my heart.

"We were all captured," he said. "They wanted to force us to convert to Islam. My hands were bound with a rope hanging from the ceiling. Then they brought in another man. He was a Coptic Christian."

"How did you know he was Coptic?" I asked.

"Because of the cross tattooed on his arm," he replied. "Only the Copts have those. They demanded, in Arabic, that he deny Christ as the Son of God. And he refused. Then they beheaded him. His blood sprinkled on the walls and landed also on my body."

As he recounted the story, the room fell into silence. After a while he said, "Nothing can shock me anymore. After what my eyes and ears have seen and heard, nothing can shock me."

"How did you escape?" I asked him.

He gave a simple reply: "A large sum was paid for my release by my Western employer, a major security firm."

It took me days to digest the further details he described to me that day, and it made me realize once again how Christ is suffering His Passion in His followers.

His story reminded me of the Christ from my childhood — the one depicted on all those crucifixes, who had watched over me in Sarleinsbach, in the classrooms, and in the old Austrian churches with their worn stone floors and candlelit altars. But He was not only there. He was everywhere. In the streets, in the mountains, at crossroads, in homes. The crucifix stood before me, with the suffering Christ, His body wounded, His head bowed in agony.

His gaze still followed me, calling me — though I did not yet understand where to truly find Him. The Jesus I had missed, the Jesus I had longed for, had never left. I had simply not yet found Him in His fullness.

Although I occasionally visited Catholic churches to look at Jesus on the Cross, there was no one to guide me, and searching for truth within the German Catholic Church felt like trying to find water in a desert. The different parishes where I was living at the time seemed completely non-missionary — there was no fire, no passion, no deep call to share the joy of loving Christ with others. It was in this wilderness that God, knowing my longing for truth, began to send me the saints.

The first voice to reach me across the centuries was St. Augustine. A journalist from *Der Spiegel* came to interview me about my life and quoted him. Struck by Augustine's words, I went to the "library of the Church Fathers" to read him for myself. His writings hit me with such force that they shattered many misconceptions I had unknowingly absorbed about Catholicism. The first time I read *Confessions*, I ran to the daughter of my Evangelical friends in whose house I was living and exclaimed, "This is the truth! Why did no one ever tell me this?"

I had always been taught that Catholicism was a later development, something that had diverged from the early Church and was foreign to the faith the Apostles had known. Yet, here was Augustine, a Father of the Church, constantly speaking of the Catholic Church. He didn't just reference the Church as a concept, he spoke of it as something real, something foundational to the Christian faith. It was impossible to ignore: The very Church I had been taught to reject was the Church Augustine himself loved and defended.

At the same time, Augustine's words about his relationship with Christ moved me deeply. Sometimes I read Augustine and couldn't help but shout in excitement at the poetic love he expressed. My friend's daughter, instead of asking if I was okay, would simply ask from a distance, "Are you reading Augustine?"

Of course I was, especially because I had been told that Catholics didn't have a personal relationship with Jesus, that their faith was bound by rituals. But Augustine's writings were filled with a burning love for Christ — a love that was poetic, personal, and alive. He was a man who had encountered Christ in a profound, intimate way, and this love was the very essence of the Catholic faith, not the empty ritualism I had been led to believe.

When I confronted my pastor — a man who used to be Catholic himself — with Augustine's writings, he insisted, "We are like the early church! Catholicism came later!" This response only sparked a deeper curiosity in me, leading me to search the writings of the Church Fathers to see when the word "Catholic" was first mentioned.

It was in the library of the Church Fathers that I discovered St. Ignatius of Antioch, whose letters took me even deeper into the heart of the early Church, revealing a perspective that continued to challenge my understanding and expand my view of the faith.

Ignatius had walked in the very footsteps of the apostles, and his writings revealed a Church far different from the fragmented, invisible body many of my Evangelical friends imagined. He didn't speak of a Church scattered across the earth with no visible authority; he spoke of a unified, tangible Church, one led by bishops who carried the apostolic flame. "Wherever Jesus Christ is, there is the Catholic Church," Ignatius declared. His Church was not an invention of later centuries — it was the Church of the apostles, the same one that had endured persecution, suffering, and martyrdom for the sake of Christ. This was the Church for which Ignatius gave his life, and it was this Church that drew me to itself.

The Church that Ignatius described was not one that shied away from suffering; it embraced it, just as Christ had embraced His Cross. This was the community of believers that had endured through the centuries, the one that carried the life and the wounds of Christ in every generation. And I began to realize that this Church — the one Ignatius and Augustine spoke of — was the Catholic Church.

When I shared these insights with my Protestant friends, many of them recoiled. The Evangelical mindset, so firmly rooted in the idea that Catholicism had no place in the early Church, simply couldn't accept the weight of history I was discovering. They still clung to the belief that the Catholic Church had strayed from the faith of the apostles, that it had "corrupted" Christianity over the centuries. But I now saw that this was not the truth. The Catholic Church was there, from the very beginning, alive and vibrant, as the true Body of Christ.

"I don't care about Ignatius or Augustine!" one of the ladies in my prayer group snapped. "I have the Bible to guide me."

She was referring to *sola scriptura* — the doctrine Martin Luther had unleashed upon the world — which was their refuge, their final word. Yet, I wondered, how could the Holy Spirit leap over centuries of wisdom, over men like Ignatius and Augustine, only to rest upon a man so deeply flawed as Luther?

Had they ever read Luther's own words? The man who had shattered the unity of Christendom, who spoke of faith yet degraded women, scorned Jews, and wallowed in his own unchecked desires? I had stood in Wartburg, where Luther had hidden and translated the Bible, and I had read his writings with my own eyes. "If the wife doesn't want to, let the maid come!" he had written with a careless laugh. "Just as I can't roll away mountains, fly with birds, create new stars, bite off my nose, I can't stop fornicating."

Was this the reformer they followed — a man whose words betrayed the very holiness he claimed to restore?

The realization struck me with force. If truth was to be found, it could not be in a doctrine that discarded the wisdom of the saints. It could not be in a faith that erased history, that denied the very structure Christ Himself had established.

Before I had the chance to truly examine Martin Luther's life, I had accepted the German Protestant vision of him: a towering, heroic reformer who had single-handedly restored the purity of the Christian faith. It was a legend I had never questioned. But then I began to read.

The deeper I dug, the more uneasy I became. Most Protestants, I realized, were just like me — they accepted the myth without ever lifting the veil. They revered him as a man of unshakable conviction, a liberator from Catholic "corruption." Yet, when I looked beyond the surface, what I found was something far darker. There were his views — his venomous words about women, his repugnant diatribes against the Jews. They reminded me, with disturbing clarity, of another historical figure I had encountered in my past: Muhammed.

In his book *On the Jews and Their Lies* (Wittenberg, 1543), Luther did not merely reject Jewish theology but issued what sounds more like a call for annihilation: "First, to set fire to their synagogues or schools and to bury and cover with dirt whatever will not burn, so that no man will ever again see a stone or cinder of them."

I felt a chill as I read those words. This was not the language of a reformer, nor of a prophet. This was the language of hatred. It came as no surprise to me that Adolf Hitler once described Martin Luther as "a great man." In *Mein Kampf*, he hailed him as "a great warrior" and a true statesman. The weight of that statement lingered in my mind like an ominous shadow. What did it mean that one of history's most notorious figures found inspiration in this so-called reformer? Had the world truly built its Protestant faith upon such a man? Had millions followed a doctrine so morally corrupt at its roots?

A fire stirred within me. Truth could not rest upon foundations so cracked, nor be found in myths or half-told histories. It had to be something else — something greater, something unbroken. Yet, as I struggled with my growing unease about Luther, a deeper and more unsettling question began to take root in my heart.

I turned to Sylvia, an Evangelical friend who had previously been Catholic, and asked her: "Could it truly be possible that God had abandoned His Church for fifteen hundred years? And if He did, where did He hide Himself? And why would the God of Love do such a thing?"

And then there was the chaos Luther had left in his wake. If the Holy Spirit had truly guided him, why did his "reformation" fracture into an ever-expanding labyrinth of contradictions? Today, there are more than forty thousand Protestant denominations, each claiming divine inspiration, yet each proclaiming something different.

"Is the Holy Spirit fragmented?" I asked. But I quickly realized that not many were eager to ask such questions. They were content with the community they had built. One friend said, "I prayed, and I received! So, God must be with us."

But I couldn't help thinking, "Maybe God answered your prayer not because of your faith, but because He knows that if He didn't, you would lose all hope in Him." Since some of their prayers were answered, they were certain God was with them and felt no need to search for the fullness of truth. Or perhaps they were simply afraid of losing the friendships the community provided.

I could not stop asking my question. It pressed upon me, relentless and unyielding. Either Christ had established a Church that endured, or He had left His followers to drift, hopelessly lost in a sea of personal interpretation. I had to know the truth.

As I reflected on the teachings of Ignatius and Augustine, it became clear to me that the truth was not something new or fractured. It was ancient, unbroken, and alive. It was the Catholic Church — the Church that had existed since the time of the apostles, the Church I had first encountered in Sarleinsbach when I arrived as a Muslim, the Church that had endured through the ages. This was the Church Christ had founded, the one that had carried the life and suffering of Christ from generation to generation. And it was this Church that I knew in my heart was home.

Soon, inspired by the writings of St. Ignatius and St. Augustine, I found myself standing at the threshold of a Catholic church near

Stuttgart, uncertain but determined. I had come to make my first Confession, though I barely understood what that meant. As I stepped into the dimly lit confessional — the "box," as some called it — I hesitated for a moment. But then, with a deep breath, I began.

I spoke simply, explaining to the priest why I was there, though the words felt foreign on my tongue. The experience was disorienting at first. The Catholic Church called certain things mortal sins that my Protestant formation had never even questioned. How could I have known? I was still a stranger in this new land, fumbling my way through unfamiliar terrain.

My conscience still carried the imprint of Protestant teachings, lingering like shadows over my soul. For years, I had been told that Catholics were idolaters, that their prayers to Mary and the saints were little more than blasphemous acts of worship. But as I reflected on my own encounters with the saints, a quiet revelation began to unfold within me.

God, in His mercy, had not left me alone in my struggles. He had surrounded me with His heavenly army — His faithful ones like Ignatius and St. Augustine, who interceded and walked beside me in unseen ways. My conversations with them were not acts of worship; they were communion. They were friendships, forged across the veil of time.

Yet, there were still barriers to overcome. A big one was Mary. "Why should I pray to Mary when I can go straight to God?" I asked the priest.

"Did God come straight to us?" he asked in reply.

"No, He came through Mary."

"Then you, too, can go to Him through Mary."

One day, sitting in the quiet of a church, I turned to God with a silent plea. *If it truly matters to You that I pray to Your mother, help me to do so.* The words were simple, but the weight of them was immense. My own relationship with my mother had been strained, and reaching out to a mother in prayer felt unnatural. But Mary, with her quiet, maternal grace, did not abandon me.

It began subtly. The Rosary — repetitive and foreign at first — gradually became something else entirely: an anchor, a lifeline. The steady rhythm of prayer wove itself into my daily life, each bead slipping through my fingers like the gentle hand of a mother guiding her child forward. And then, one day, the truth struck me with unmistakable clarity: Just as Islam has no father, Protestantism has no mother.

Yet, at the foot of the Cross, in His final act of love, Christ gave us His own mother. "Behold your mother," He said to John, and to all of us. And so, I took her hand, clinging to the Rosary, allowing her to lead me ever closer to her Son.

My Protestant friends couldn't understand. Many of them had once been Catholics, and in that, I saw a great tragedy. The Catholicism they had left behind was not the fullness of faith — it was a distorted, watered-down version of it. Perhaps they had never been properly taught as children. What troubled me more, however, was that instead of seeking a deeper understanding or wrestling with the full depth of the faith, they had chosen the easier path — the path away.

As I continued to search for truth, an unexpected invitation arrived: A priest from Austria, a member of a Traditional Latin Mass community, contacted me and asked if I would speak to his parishioners. Without hesitation, I agreed.

When I finally met Fr. Bernard, a young priest clad in a simple black soutane, he looked at me with a mix of surprise and amusement. "I didn't think you'd reply when I sent my message," he confessed. "You're famous. Why would you come to my little parish?"

What he didn't know was that I was desperate for guidance, yearning for a deeper connection within the Church. And so, I had come — not to speak, but to seek.

It had been eleven years since my Baptism into the Catholic Church. The priest who had baptized me never mentioned that I needed to be confirmed, nor had any other priests subsequently. It was Fr. Bernard who in his unyielding way explained it to me.

He was unlike any priest I had ever met before — deeply informed about Islam and deeply concerned about its rapid growth. He didn't just acknowledge the struggles of converts; he worked to help them. His parish regularly held Eucharistic Adoration for the conversion of Muslims, he never missed an opportunity to pray for persecuted Christians, and he encouraged his congregation to remember their duty to stand with those suffering for Christ's sake.

His faith wasn't just words; it was action.

"Do I need catechism classes?" I asked. He laughed and replied, "No, you should be teaching them!"

Still, I felt I needed them, so I went to a Cistercian monastery to learn from monks who lived a strict life of penance and prayer, in order to prepare myself for entering the Catholic Church.

After that, Fr. Bernard introduced me to the bishop. Now, eleven years after my Baptism into the Catholic Church, the bishop confirmed me in his beautiful private chapel, which reminded me of the ones I had often seen in Sarleinsbach.[6] Then I returned to Germany, absolutely on fire with the Holy Spirit. People kept telling me that I should wait and see if someone was ready to hear about Jesus before bringing Him up. The problem? I was *always* ready to talk about Jesus! Every conversation, every quiet moment, somehow turned into me rambling about my newfound best friends: St. Augustine and St. Ignatius of Antioch — those ancient voices that had finally led me home to the Catholic Church.

But my zeal was soon met with a sobering truth: Religious like Fr. Bernard were rare in Europe. One afternoon, in my local church, I saw

---

[6] Confirmation is one of the seven sacraments of the Catholic Church. It is the process through which a baptized person is sealed with the gift of the Holy Spirit. This sacrament strengthens and deepens one's faith, marking the individual as a mature member of the Church. It often follows Baptism and is considered a step toward fully embracing the responsibilities of being a Catholic. The bishop typically administers this sacrament through the laying on of hands and anointing with oil, symbolizing the strengthening of the Holy Spirit within the person.

a religious sister and, eager to share my joy, approached her. I spoke to her with unguarded enthusiasm, recounting the wisdom of St. Ignatius, the depth of his devotion to the Eucharist, the certainty with which he proclaimed the Real Presence. She listened, nodding absently, her face unreadable. Then, with a soft sigh, she shook her head.

"It doesn't matter which congregation you belong to," she said lightly. "I receive the Eucharist at both Protestant and Catholic churches. Jesus loves everyone."

Her words, meant perhaps to reassure, struck me like a distant bell tolling, soft but profound. A chasm had opened between us — one not of enmity but of misunderstanding. I had expected joyful acceptance and the spark of shared faith. Maybe even a great welcome like the Muslims give to Christians when they choose Islam. Instead, I stood alone in my certainty while the Catholic sister smiled, seemingly untouched by the fire that burned in me.

With a weary shake of her head, she dismissed me. She had spent years helping mold the Church into something more "welcoming," more modern, smoothing down its rough edges until nothing remained to challenge or disturb. In her eyes, converts like me — zealous, insistent, and unwilling to accept a diluted faith — were nothing but an inconvenience and an irritation. She did not want to be disturbed.

But I did. I longed for a faith that burned, that purified, that demanded everything and returned even more. And I needed a spiritual family that cared.

At that time, I was drowning in grief. My grandfather had passed away in Pakistan, and only months later was I informed about it. I learned that, in his final moments, he had longed to hear my voice one last time. The weight of that knowledge crushed me, pressing against my chest like an unbearable burden. It became a silent wound that no word of comfort could reach.

Still, that day — like every day — I attended the Holy Sacrifice of the Mass, even as life weighed heavily on me. And then, something extraordinary happened — something so deeply personal that I cannot share it publicly. It was an experience beyond words, beyond expression.

A few times, at the urging of my spiritual director, I have tried to write it down. But each time I read what I had written or attempted to articulate in words, it felt inadequate — like mere shadows of the reality I had encountered. Worse, I feared that even trying to describe it might offend God, as if I were reducing something sacred to mere human language.

What I *can* say is this: For years, the image of the man on the Cross, His suffering gaze, the Jesus of my childhood and beyond, had been leading me here — to the actual *Presence* of His Sacrifice on the Cross. I realized, in a way deeper than ever before, that there is no path to Him except through the Cross. Not just the memory of the Cross or the burdens we carry in life, but *His* Cross — His Passion, eternally offered to the Father.

Christ does not stand apart from His Cross; He places it between us and Himself. His redemptive act is not merely a past event in history — it is ever-present. For years, His presence everywhere — on the mountainsides, in the classroom, in my moments of prayer — was pointing me to this one truth. The Sacrifice of the Cross is not confined to time; it is still here, renewed and made present at every Mass.

The Sacrifice of the Mass and the Cross are inseparable, each a reflection of the other. The Mass, at its core, is sacrificial. To love is to give — completely, without reserve, even to the point of death. This is the love of the Cross, the love that transforms and redeems. And in the Mass, that love is not only remembered; it is continually *offered* to us, that we might enter into it.

One of my Evangelical friends, Valerie, told me, "Jesus died on the Cross. To be saved, all you have to do is believe it."

I answered with something that I had heard another convert say: "But doesn't the devil also believe that Jesus died on the Cross? And yet, he is not saved by it."

She hesitated before asking, "Are you saying Christ's death on the Cross wasn't sufficient? That He is still dying in the Mass?"

No. The power of the Cross does not need to be *completed*, but rather *applied*. What she had was the *memory* of Christ's death. But what happens in the Mass is more than just a remembrance — it is the making present of that single, eternal act of redemption, brought to us beyond time. I'm not a theologian, but this is how I understood it.

Valerie and my other Protestant friends wrestled with the choices I made. They struggled to understand why I left Wittenberg for Rome, why I yoked myself to an ancient Church that, to them, seemed like little more than a relic of the past. Valerie even scoffed: "What's so attractive about the Catholic Church? You sit in a building full of eighty-year-old women with nothing to offer you."

I spoke to her about truth — the kind of truth that doesn't bend to time, that doesn't shift with culture, that doesn't seek to please but seeks to sanctify — and of course about the Sacrifice of the Mass. Intrigued, she bought books by St. Augustine and a copy of *Summa Theologica*, wrestling with its towering logic like a fighter sparring with a ghost. Then, one day, without a word to me, she slipped into a Catholic Mass.

Her experience left her shaken.

"When it was time for Communion," she confessed later, "I went up and crossed my arms, just as you told me to if I were ever to go to Mass, but the priest tried to give me the Eucharist anyway. I told him I wasn't Catholic, but he insisted. He said that Jesus comes to everyone!" She returned to her pew, staring at the Host in bewilderment.

"You tell me Protestants have so many denominations, while your Church professes one faith everywhere," she said. "But you don't. Your Church is divided too."

And she was right.

The parish I attended in Germany mirrored the decline of many Catholic churches in the country: small, gray-haired, and weighed down by the air of resignation. A woman regularly delivered the homily, her voice a dull murmur against the heavy silence of forgotten tradition. The congregation, uncertain and untethered, sat through the liturgy, unsure when to kneel, hesitant about when to rise. If the priest failed to appear, extraordinary ministers distributed Communion like bread from a soup kitchen.

I remembered how, as a young girl in Dhadar, the mosque used to be filled with deep reverence. We knelt, we prayed — though Allah was worshipped only spiritually, there was a profound sense of the sacred.

But in this parish church, even though God was truly present, His presence wasn't reflected in His followers. If I had walked in as a Muslim, I would have doubted that it was truly a house of God with Christ Himself present, because there was a lack of reverence, and no one seemed to act as if He were there. The priest, a kind but timid man, seemed caught in the quiet tragedy of his own fear. He lacked the courage to defend the truth. He feared that if he spoke boldly, he would anger his congregation, and if they left, his already dwindling church would wither to nothing. So he remained silent.

I could not understand it.

How could these people — who had known Jesus for so much longer than I — be so indifferent to Him? How could one claim to love Christ yet not long to remain with Him? The less they prayed, the more I prayed in their place, as if my devotion could somehow fill the abyss of their apathy.

"I understand why you spend hours here praying," a kind Catholic woman once remarked to me. "That's how you endure your life!"

"Partially true," I replied with a smile. "In reality, I come here to console Jesus, who is betrayed by His friends."

Her elderly mother, who was standing next to me, gasped. "That's why we need more Muslim converts! None of us think that way!"

Then, after a series of profound and extraordinary spiritual experiences — ones too personal for words — Fr. Bernard extended another invitation. He suggested I consider the religious life. Without hesitation,

I accepted and went on retreat, eager to discern my calling. I wanted to give everything to Christ. I wanted to offer the greatest thing I possibly could for Him.

But as I prayed, the answer came — not in a whisper, but in the certainty of fire. I had already been called, not to the cloister, but to the Passion.

Christ had chosen me to console Him in His Passion by helping those who are persecuted for His sake. My mission is to be the Veronica who meets Him on the way to Calvary, to show Him acts of love when He is mocked, beaten and broken by the heaviness of the Cross. The greatest thing I could do was not to embrace the religious life but to suffer with Him for the sake of righteousness and truth.

14

LOSING EUROPE

ONCE I BEGAN speaking out publicly about Islam, my days in Europe were numbered. I had been on the run ever since I left my family, and the more I spoke out, the more dangerous my situation became.

In 2015, I released my third book, *Sharia in Germany*, which quickly climbed *Der Spiegel*'s bestseller list. The book shed light on the parallel judicial system established by Sharia law in Germany and how radical Muslims were exploiting it to erode democratic values. At the time, I was still living under victims' protection in the little village near Stuttgart, but the danger only intensified as I continued publicly to speak out about the abuse of Christians in refugee shelters and the mistreatment of women in Islam.

I soon started noticing Muslim men following me — to church, through the streets. At one of my lectures, a group of bearded Salafists — with long robes swaying, their expression dark — entered the hall, flanked by veiled women cloaked in black. The sight of them sent a ripple of unease through the audience, but I refused to be intimidated. Every time I started to speak, they would shout, "Not true! Not true!" I looked the Salafists in the eye and told them why I had chosen Jesus over Muhammed.

"A woman caught in adultery was brought before Jesus, and He showed her mercy. A woman caught in adultery was brought before Muhammed, and He demanded that she be stoned."

One of the Salafists stood up abruptly. His face twisted in anger as he stalked toward me. A chill swept through the room. The audience recoiled, fear gripping them. Before he could reach me, security intervened, rushing me out through the back. The next day's lecture was canceled. Those who had invited me no longer felt safe.

Every public appearance I made now required police or security protection. While I fought for the freedom of others, my own was slowly slipping away. Fear followed me, even when I used public transportation. At train stations, they would wait, calling out my name — "Sabatina James!" — and insulting me.

When I reported these incidents to one of my police protection officers, he explained, "They do this to warn you — to show that they can get close whenever they want."

During some of my church visits, two armed guards would stand at the entrance, a silent reminder that freedom of religion was no longer guaranteed in Germany.

"Why doesn't the Catholic Church help you?" my friends would ask.

The answer of course is that the Church in the West does not offer people like me a place of refuge. One day, when I attended Holy Mass, the deacon ascended the pulpit. His voice, measured and solemn, echoed through the space, each word heavy with conviction. He spoke of love — of bridges to be built, of walls to be torn down. He urged the congregation to welcome Muslim immigration into Germany, calling it an act of kindness, a duty of mercy, a reflection of Christ's boundless embrace. It was, he insisted, the will of Pope Francis himself.[7]

---

[7] Pope Francis would formalize his position in 2019, in a joint declaration signed in Abu Dhabi with Sunni authority and grand imam of al-Azhar, Sheikh Ahmed el-Tayeb, who upholds al-Azhar's doctrine advocating the execution of those who abandon Islam.

Titled *A Document on Human Fraternity for World Peace and Living Together* — though known more simply as the Abu Dhabi document — the declaration opens by asserting that its authors are promulgating it "in the name of God." This implies a common belief in the same God, with the same name. However, Catholics profess belief in the Holy Trinity, three divine Persons — Father, Son, and Holy

The weight of his proclamation pressed down on my chest. There I sat — a survivor of persecution, a fugitive from a world that sought my silence, a woman living under the watchful eye of police because of the very ideology that the Holy Father Pope Francis now invited in with open arms. How easily these Catholics spoke of love, of peace, of unity, as if such things could be conjured by wishful thinking alone.

They did not know. How could they? They had never watched friends disappear into the abyss of Islamic jihad. They had never stood before the face of a jihadi and been marked for death because of the truth they dared to proclaim.

I recall a religious sister once saying, "You just have to trust in God and not be afraid. I have no fears about the future." But why would she? She has never risked anything for the truth, never defended Christ when His gospel was scorned by Muslims. It is always striking how those who have never encountered real danger because of their faith feel so entitled to offer advice on courage. They resemble Job's friends: well-intentioned, perhaps, but entirely detached from the harsh realities of faith under threat.

For me, danger had been a constant companion. I had broken with Sharia for the sake of truth, and that choice had consequences.

Spirit — in one God, while Islam rejects this doctrine. In fact, Islam considers belief in the Trinity to be the greatest sin, as it is viewed as *shirk* — the act of associating partners with God. In Islamic theology, *shirk* is regarded as the severe offense of compromising belief in the absolute oneness of God (*Tawhid*). By invoking "the name of God," the joint declaration suggests that there is no significant difference between the way the two religions view nature and identity of God.

The Abu Dhabi document also asserts that "faith leads a believer to see in the other a brother or sister to be supported and loved." But such a premise not only fails to distinguish between the supernatural gift of Christian faith and the merely natural belief of all other religions but also turns a blind eye to Islam's views on women, "nonbelievers," and jihad. Furthermore, its claim that "the pluralism and the diversity of religions [are] willed by God in His wisdom" not only reduces Christianity but leads one to ask: "What is the point of converting?"

One evening, while traveling to meet a journalist at Hamburg's train station, I became aware of a man watching me. For many years I was assigned a police protection officer through the *Opferschutz*, a program designed to provide protection and support to victims of violence. The program's goal was to ensure my safety and help me navigate the complex legal and emotional aftermath of the crimes I had experienced. It's run by a division within the Hamburg police that works closely with victim protection services, offering specialized care for those at risk of further harm. Depending on the situation, they might provide officers for counseling, legal advice, or even relocation support, all tailored to the severity of the threat.

For me, this was a crucial safeguard, a necessary shield as I faced a world that had become unpredictable and, at times, frightening. "Never assume. You never know why a man is looking," my protection officer once said to me.

But this time it was different. As I waited for my train, the man watching me suddenly marched toward me, his voice rising above the noise of the station. There was a sense of urgency in his tone, something in his demeanor that told me this moment was unlike any other.

"You! Stop criticizing the Prophet!"

People turned to look. His fury mounted with every step, his fists clenched at his sides. I tried to reason with him, but my words only fueled his rage. Then, just as he closed the distance, another train arrived. I jumped on board at the last second, the doors sealing shut behind me. Through the window, I watched him scream, his face contorted in fury as the platform blurred into the distance.

I called the journalist I was supposed to meet that day and asked him to pick me up at the next train station. He worked for a public television station in Hamburg and had done several pieces on my efforts to help victims of forced marriage. When I told him what just happened and how thankful I was to God that the train had arrived, he responded, "God and I aren't on the best terms." Then, after a moment, he added, "But after everything you've been through, I'll believe anything you say."

Muslim men like the one who threatened me at the train station take great pride in their faith. They don't whisper it or apologize for it. In their eyes, critics of Islam must be silenced — or worse, killed.

Public transportation was not safe for me anymore. Nor was it for many German women, as it turned out. On New Year's Eve 2015, in Cologne, something horrifying happened. A large group of men, reportedly more than a thousand, gathered at the city's central train station, a major transit point located by the famous Catholic cathedral. The station was bustling with people traveling between the fireworks display and local nightclubs. The men, whom the police chief described as "Arab or North African," surrounded women, groped them, stole their belongings, and sexually abused or raped them.

This "Night of Shame," as some called it, ignited debates about multiculturalism. However, Germany continued to accept more refugees. In response to the assault, Cologne's mayor, Henriette Reker, had a piece of advice for all women: Maintain "an arm's length" distance from foreigners.

"No, send them back!" I argued on a TV show, but for a nation like Germany, which is still suffering from guilt for its past, the issue was not just political but also psychological. While no country in the world is free from historical wrongdoing, European nations are unique in their belief that they must be punished for the crimes of their ancestors. This stands in stark contrast to the Muslim world, where atrocities — such as the genocides committed against Christians — are rarely even acknowledged.

Take, for example, the Ottoman Empire. For six hundred years, it expanded across North Africa, the Middle East, and parts of Europe. In the twentieth century, it was responsible for one of the greatest atrocities in human history: the Armenian Genocide, in which more than a million Armenians were murdered by the Turks. Yet, this crime is seldom discussed, and there is no collective sense of guilt imposed on Turkey or its people.

European nations, on the other hand, engage in a culture of guilt, holding themselves accountable for past misdeeds in a way no other civilization does. This raises the question: Why is this phenomenon exclusive to the West? The selective emphasis on historical guilt suggests an anti-Western narrative rather than a genuine pursuit of justice. The Western self-flagellation continued, even though the continent faced countless other crises.

On Friday, November 13, 2015, Paris was rocked by a series of co-ordinated attacks carried out by ISIS, highlighting the ongoing threats facing Europe today. Gunmen and suicide bombers struck a concert hall, a major stadium, and restaurants and bars almost simultaneously, leaving 130 people dead and hundreds more wounded.

I could not stand by and watch. With a group of like-minded Christians from the Middle East, I had already founded *Al Hayat* (The Life), a YouTube channel dedicated to exposing the teachings of Islam — something that Muslims are not used to. It quickly gained traction, not only among those who cherished freedom but also among the very jihadis who sought to silence us. Our videos were often removed by YouTube and, after protests, reloaded again. The cost of speaking the truth was high. The question now was how much higher it would go.

To speak against Islam in the West was to step into a storm, unarmed and alone. It was not merely a matter of debate or discourse, as with other religions. No, to question Islam — its doctrines, its history, its laws — was to invite a wrath that was swift, merciless, and often deadly.

The handful of critics of Islam in Europe did not live ordinary lives. They moved from safe house to safe house, their addresses unknown even to friends. They spoke in hushed tones, glancing over their shoulders, knowing that at any moment a blade might find their throat or a bullet their heart. Police protection became their shadow, but even that was no guarantee of safety. Some had to flee their homelands altogether, living in exile as outcasts, hunted by those who had once been their neighbors. Others were not so fortunate.

There were those who dared to write, to speak, to expose the uncomfortable truths. Their names were etched into death lists circulated in the dark corners of the Internet, where radicals whispered and plotted. They were branded as blasphemers, as enemies of Allah, and in the minds of their pursuers, there was only one fitting punishment: death.

Some were gunned down in broad daylight, their blood staining the cobblestone streets of European capitals, much like the 2015 Charlie Hebdo massacre, where gunmen targeted the satirical newspaper's office over controversial cartoons depicting the Prophet Muhammed. Others were hacked to death in their own homes, the walls bearing silent witness to the fury of their executioners. And yet, the world turned away. Governments, newspapers, even fellow intellectuals spoke only in murmurs, if they spoke at all. Fear had done its work.

But perhaps the most insidious weapon was not the assassin's knife or the terrorist's bomb, but the accusation: *Islamophobe.* The word was wielded like a cudgel, meant to silence, to shame, to isolate. To be called an Islamophobe was to be cast out of polite society, to lose a career, a reputation, even friendships. The fear of that single word was often enough to keep mouths shut and pens still.

And so, the danger grew.

Every silencing of a courageous voice contributed to the shaping of a new reality — one where fear dictated speech, where truth was left unspoken, and where those who dared to resist knew they were playing a game in which the stakes were life and death.

Even politicians were not safe. In the Netherlands, Geert Wilders lived under constant guard. Ayaan Hirsi Ali, once a Somali refugee, had risen to speak out against the treatment of women under Islam, only to find herself a hunted woman, forced to flee from country to country, her life reduced to a series of locked doors and bodyguards.

And then there were already lessons learned from those who did not run. Theo van Gogh had stood defiant, refusing to bow to fear. He made a film exposing the abuse of women in Islam. One morning, as he cycled through the streets of Amsterdam, a Muslim man stepped forward and drove a knife into his chest. Then another. And another. When the body was found, the blade of a small dagger had been used to pin a note to his corpse. A warning. A promise of more blood to come. The message was clear: Criticize Islam, and you will pay in flesh.

In my case, hate messages flooded in from faceless radicals, their usernames as impersonal as their threats were visceral. "We will stone you to death!" "Heads will roll!"

These extremists wanted to silence me — and YouTube helped them do it. Our channel was taken down.

While YouTube permits jihadi channels that spread hate and allow violence to flourish, it continues to suppress dissenting voices. In doing so, it effectively aids the global media campaign led by Muslim radicals. Despite our continued efforts to produce content, YouTube repeatedly deleted our videos. Meanwhile, jihadis exploited Google's copyright dispute system, using legal loopholes to access the personal data of *Al Hayat*'s creators. We warned Google about the consequences, but they chose not to listen.

Then an email arrived, addressed to my colleague, in Arabic. The message was chilling in its simplicity: "Thank you for your personal data; it will be posted along with an image of your sender *Al Hayat* TV Net on the blacklist of al-Qaeda and other European jihadis. On the channel, you insult the Prophet, the Prophet of Islam. *Watch your head and have your house guarded by police!*"

The authorities stepped in and began investigating. Soon after receiving my final death threat I left Europe, while those who threatened me remain there — unharmed, free, and untouched.

I frequently wonder how long this can go on. For more than two decades now, Europeans have watched the streets they once called their own grow unfamiliar, their traditions eroded, their voices silenced. And still, they say nothing. They bow their heads, they whisper in private, but few dare to speak aloud the truth that gnaws at them.

The enemies of Christ — the ones who preach hatred in mosques, who attack the weak, who defile and destroy — walk freely through the streets of Vienna, Berlin, Paris, and Rome. Salafists, Hamas supporters, those who chant for blood and celebrate terror, live without fear. But those of us who defend the West and its people, who warn of what is coming, are hunted like criminals. We are forced to flee, cast out from the very civilization we are trying to protect.

There are nights when I lie awake, staring at the ceiling, lost in the memories of a childhood that feels as distant as a fairy tale. I see Austria — the snow-capped peaks, the sound of church bells ringing through the valley, the warmth of its people. But then, I wonder: *Will there come a day when Austrians themselves will speak of their country as if it were only a story? When they will say, with sorrow in their voices, "Once upon a time, there was Austria?"* Will the people of this continent — who have already begun to feel like strangers in their own lands — one day wake up and whisper into the silence, "Once upon a time, there was Europe"?

By then, will it be too late? When I arrived in Austria as a child in 1992, I still felt that Christ was the heartbeat of Europe. But it was the older generation, like Frieda and my teachers, who still carried a sense of pride in their spiritual heritage. They understood that the culture they inherited was not the product of a government but a spiritual legacy — a mustard seed planted long ago, with the voice of Jesus and the apostles as its foundation. Since then, especially as that generation has passed away, I've witnessed the fading of the heart of Jesus they once carried. And when the heart stops beating, the body dies. With the decline of Catholicism in Europe, we've seen a corresponding decline and privatization of morality. People now have their own truths and values. A society so fragmented will not be able to integrate a culture so strong and confident as Islam.

I am convinced that the future of Europe will not be decided at the roundtables of the European Union. Instead, it will be determined on the streets of Europe, and it won't be pretty.

15

THE RETREAT

THE TRAGEDY OF Europe lies not only in the fact that it has replaced the next generation with Muslim migrants, but that the Muslims arrived precisely at a time when Europe had lost the faith upon which it was built. In 2015, Angela Merkel, Germany's conservative chancellor, made a choice that would change the course of European history forever: She opened Germany's doors to a flood of refugees. The migrants Merkel allowed into Germany claimed to be fleeing terror, and some probably were, particularly from the Islamic State in Iraq and Syria (ISIS).

Yet, it was the most persecuted groups — the Christians and Yazidis, who had been the first targets of ISIS — that rarely made it across Europe's borders. Ironically, some of the very same Muslims who claimed to flee Syria, Iraq, and Afghanistan because of Islamic violence were now enforcing the strict Islamic rules on Christian refugees in Germany.

I'll never forget the day I met a Pakistani Catholic living in an asylum home near Munich. He showed me his injuries. "They — Muslim asylum seekers — wanted me to take off my cross. When I refused, they took off their belts and beat me with them," he explained.

"Have you spoken to the police?" I asked.

"No," he replied, his voice heavy with fear. "I'm too scared. The other Muslims might testify against me, and I'm alone in this."

"What about the priest? Have you spoken to the church nearby?" I inquired.

"Yes," he said, "I went there. The priest told me to visit the cardinal's office. So I went, sat there, and waited. But the cardinal's secretary told me he doesn't have time for me."

I was speechless.

One of my Evangelical friends suggested to me, "Why don't you write a letter to the bishops yourself? They know who you are. Maybe they'll listen."

So I decided to contact nearly every German bishop and cardinal I had ever heard of with a straightforward request: "Will you meet with the persecuted Christians?" Not in Pakistan. Not in Afghanistan. Not in Syria. But in the very dioceses these bishops had vowed to protect.

Not a single one was willing. While I was deeply disheartened, I am neither surprised nor scandalized by the indifference of the bishops. Through their actions, these men of God are disfiguring the Church — the Body of Christ — causing Him pain with their sins. At times, when my friends witnessed the behavior of the clergy, they chose to leave the Church. But to me, that felt like abandoning Jesus on the Cross, where His body — already bruised and torn by the sins of mankind — was further wounded by those who should have remained faithful.

Over the years I have realized something vital: The Catholic Church, though imperfect and wounded in her human element by the sins of her members, is still the Body of Christ. Just as Christ's body was disfigured and broken, so too is His Church, but that does not diminish her sacredness because Christ and the Church are one. The wounds inflicted upon His Body by the bishops do not change her essence. In the face of this suffering, I am drawn closer to Him, vowing to remain faithful, just as Mary and John remained at the foot of the Cross when others fled.

To walk away from the Church is to walk away from Jesus Himself.

Our Lord's final prayer was that all of us might be one: "I pray … that they may all be one, as you, Father, are in me and I in you"

(John 17:20–21, NABRE). Jesus never intended for us to abandon the Church when it becomes difficult or uncomfortable. The Church is His Body, and while many cells may be sick, abandoning the Body is not the answer. The answer is to become healthy cells ourselves — renewing the Church, not by walking away, but by committing to holiness, living lives of virtue, and faithfully following the gospel.

I remain Catholic because I believe, without hesitation, in the truth of Christ's teachings and in the profound supernatural grace bestowed through the sacraments. To walk away from it, to seek a church that conforms more to my desires, is to deny the truth. If I were to leave the Catholic Church for a spiritual community that better aligns with my preferences, I would not be seeking Jesus and His Church, but only myself.

Europe's ecclesial institutions have undergone a profound transformation in recent years. Once central to the continent's moral and spiritual life, they've increasingly abandoned their core mission of preaching the gospel. I once became deeply frustrated when, in my own church, secular issues such as climate change and interreligious dialogue were treated as the most urgent matters. Unable to stay silent, I went to the priest and asked, "What did Jesus ask you to do? Don't you think saving souls should be your priority?" My outburst clearly took him by surprise. But this wasn't just a personal frustration — it reflects a larger shift happening across Europe, where religion has gradually lost its central place in public life.

While some argue the Church is adapting to modern concerns, the reality is that this focus on politics and activism comes at the expense of faith. High-ranking prelates and clergy seem ready to sacrifice the uniqueness of the Catholic Church in their eagerness to remain relevant in an increasingly secular society. The danger is clear: By prioritizing secular causes over spiritual ones, these prelates have not only cast aside the supernatural but also alienated the very people the Church is meant to serve, leaving them searching for meaning in a world that increasingly seems indifferent to faith.

Coupled with this, for many years European politicians warned their people of a "population explosion" and the imminent threat of climate change. They urged families to have fewer children, to be mindful of the burden too many people would place on the planet. And then, almost overnight, the message changed. Suddenly, there weren't enough children. The future was uncertain, and the next generation needed to be replaced. The solution, they said, lay beyond their borders. The answer was immigration — waves of newcomers from distant lands, many from Muslim-majority countries.

Before throwing open Europe's doors to the entire Muslim world, wouldn't it have made sense to first consider whether there were policies that could encourage their own people to have more children? To revive the declining birthrates, to restore faith in the future? But instead, European leaders looked elsewhere.

Rather than nurture the next generation from within, they chose to import it from another continent. It was easier, perhaps — more immediate, more practical in their eyes. A solution without the need for reflection. But beneath the surface, the questions lingered: Was Muslim mass immigration an attempt to de-Christianize Europe? Was it an attack on Christ Himself?

A recent study revealed that Muslims have now become the largest religious group in Vienna's primary schools, outnumbering Catholics.

The situation is no different in other parts of Western Europe. If the current migration trend continues, Pew Research projects that about 31 percent of Swedes will be Muslim by mid-century. Migration is also a key factor in the projected growth of the Muslim populations in other Western European countries, including France and the United Kingdom. In the midterm scenario, both France and the U.K. are expected to have Muslim populations of around 17 percent by 2050.

In some schools in Germany and Austria, 90 percent of students under eighteen are immigrants, and most of them are Muslims. Out of fear for the safety of their children, some of my own friends have left the bigger cities and retreated to rural areas where Christian culture still exists in pockets. But how long will it take until the next influx of refugees are placed in their village? In certain areas of Germany, there are hardly any German children to be seen anywhere. And even where there are, soon enough they will be a minority. Once Muslim migrant groups become strong and confident enough, they demand that Sharia be implemented in their schools, and the Christian children have to obey.

Recent years have seen many episodes that reveal an increasingly emboldened Islam. In Vienna there was an incident where Muslim students smashed a crucifix, tore pages out of the Bible in the classroom, and then urinated on it. Then they threw the Bible in the garbage. Not one priest, bishop, or cardinal protested this sacrilegious and disgraceful attack, even though the school principal, Christian Klar, went public with the story. In a TV interview titled "Influence of Islam in Austrian School Grows," he said:

> In my school, the Islamic perspective is the predominant one. One time, the children came to school during Ramadan and told me that one of the Austrian kids is now a Muslim too. And that he had to fast. The Austrian child agreed he had left Christianity. When I called his mother, a devout Catholic who prays the Rosary regularly, she was utterly shocked to learn that her son had converted to Islam.

Such incidents have happened across every European country and have often gone beyond peaceful proselytizing. In city after city, violence has erupted in various forms.

In Britain, for example, Muslim men targeted children. Their victims were working-class English girls, who were lured, drugged, and passed around like toys. The numbers were staggering, thousands of victims. One girl who spoke out said: "I was raped by over a thousand men!"

And the worst part? The truth had been buried for years. Police knew. Social workers knew. But fear paralyzed them. No one wanted to be labeled a racist. No one dared speak against the perpetrators, because they were mostly Muslim men of Pakistani origin. And so, the rapes continued. The abuse spanned decades. Some girls were injected with dangerous doses of heroin by their abusers. One girl who was injected with an overdose of heroine did not survive.

It was the largest-scale sexual exploitation of working-class white girls in modern British history. And yet, even when the truth finally broke, no one dared acknowledge the obvious: These girls were targeted precisely because they were *not* Muslim.

Meanwhile, Muslim activists were trying to convince the public that this was not in conformity with Islam. But why not? Were these child-abusers doing anything that Muhammed had not done? Did he not have sex-slaves? Did he not marry a six-year-old?

The Koran, in sura 4:24, explicitly tells Muslim men to have as many non-Muslim sex-slaves as pleases them: "And forbidden to you are wedded wives of other people except those whom your right hand possesses [captives of Dar al-Harb, i.e., the house of war]." This verse is part of a larger passage that addresses the women Muslim men are permitted to marry or have sexual relations with. The phrase "captives whom your right hand possesses" refers to slave women owned by Muslim men.

While I am horrified at the violence these poor girls had to endure, I am not surprised. In fact, I am more surprised that everyone else is so surprised. After all, this is the violence that little Christian girls endure each day in countries like Pakistan, where more than a thousand Christian and Hindu girls are abducted and sexually exploited by Muslim men every year. In one case, the victim was a twelve-year-old Catholic girl named Shazia Bashir, who was raped and then brutally murdered by Chaudry Naeem, an influential lawyer. My colleague in Pakistan, who was there when the body of the victim was collected, remarked, "There were traces of torture all over her body!"

After the raping, torturing, and killing Shazia, the police officers at the Litton Road police station in Pakistan, where Shazia's mother reported the brutal murder, refused to investigate the crime, telling her mother that "a case against a lawyer cannot be registered."

Meanwhile, back in Europe, Muslim apologists were actively trying to convince Western audiences that this version of Islam wasn't the authentic one but simply a perversion of their faith. The question, then, to be raised is: Why didn't any Muslims protest when Shazia was raped and murdered? Why are Pakistani imams constantly against laws banning kidnapping and forced marriages and conversions? Where are the hundreds and thousands on the streets of London to protest the rape of British girls? The truth is that they must know that the abusers were faithfully following the example of the Prophet Muhammed.

The abuse of girls and women is not the only threat that the rising tide of Muslim immigration has brought into Europe. Violence against those who were already a minority within a minority — the most vulnerable of all, those who had chosen to leave Islam — has risen sharply. Few knew this better than Nissar Hussain, a man of extraordinary courage.

A father of six, Nissar had long endured harassment from his Muslim neighbors in the U.K. They saw his conversion to Christianity as a betrayal, an offense punishable not just in their eyes, but according to the words of their prophet: "If someone leaves Islam, kill him." And they tried. Repeatedly.

One evening, two hooded men lay in wait. When Nissar stepped outside, they struck. Armed with a pickax handle, they beat him to the ground, shattering his kneecap and breaking his hand. The assault was captured on CCTV, yet that did nothing to deter further violence.

His car was destroyed. His house was nearly set on fire. And still, the authorities hesitated.

When he turned to the Anglican church for help, pleading with its bishops for protection, their response was one of appeasement. Dialogue, peace, interfaith understanding — these were their priorities, not the suffering of a man who had chosen Christ. The Anglican church echoed the same message Pope Francis had preached in 2016 when, during Holy Week, he washed the feet of Muslim migrants. Meanwhile, Nissar was forced to flee his home for a second time with his six children. Armed police arrived without warning, gathered what his family could carry, and relocated them far from Bradford.

In a phone call with me he said that he felt lonely because the Christians in his church didn't understand the weight of his suffering: "Can these people even imagine how hard it is to go through all of this, especially when your children are still in school and university, and you are suddenly being forced to leave your family home?" I told him not to wait for the church and its members, as his persecution is either beyond their imagination or below their interest.

And where is the Catholic Church? Unfortunately, it finds itself on the wrong side. During his 2014 visit to Turkey, Pope Francis referred to the Koran as "a prophetic book of peace." In response, a group of Muslim converts wrote an open letter to the pope, pleading with him to recognize their struggles and addressing him directly, "If Islam is a good religion, as you teach, why did we become Catholic? Many of us are even afraid to sign our names to this letter, fearing for our lives. Why do you not even answer our letters?"

To the best of my knowledge, Pope Francis never responded.

Ex-Muslim converts to the faith will find no refuge in the very place that should have been their final stronghold. The Catholic Church, once the great citadel of Christendom, has long since laid down her arms before Islam.

There was, perhaps, a single tremor in this — a fleeting moment when truth, unshackled, nearly slipped past careful lips. In Regensburg, Pope Benedict XVI, a man of scholarly precision, dared to quote the Byzantine emperor Manuel II Palaiologos: "Show me just what Muhammed brought that was new and there you will find things only evil and inhuman spread by the sword and the faith that he preached." The Holy Father did not endorse these words but only repeated them, wrapping them in disclaimers, qualifying them with caution. Twice in his speech, he distanced himself from them, calling the emperor's remarks "brusque" and "unacceptable." But no amount of hesitancy could shield him from what followed.

The storm was swift and merciless. Across the Islamic world there were riots; crosses burned and churches smoldered in a wake of violent reprisals. Blood was spilled in places where the papal words had never even been heard. A sixty-five-year-old Italian nun was murdered in Somalia. What followed was telling.

Instead of defending his position, the pope said that he was "deeply sorry" about offending the sensitivity of Muslims. Mahmoud Ashour, the former deputy of Cairo's Al-Azhar Mosque, the most influential institution in the Sunni Arab world, told Al-Arabiya TV right after the pope's speech, "This is not enough. He should offer an apology for insulting the beliefs of Islam. He must apologize openly and admit his mistake." Immediately a delegation was sent to meet with Muslim leaders, and within months, Pope Benedict found himself visiting the Blue Mosque in Istanbul, standing in silent prayer alongside an imam. The message was clear: The Church had no courage to challenge Islam.

Benedict's successor had taken heed. Cardinal Jorge Bergoglio — soon to be Pope Francis — did not merely remain silent. He rebuked Benedict, calling upon fellow Catholics to do the same, to chastise their own pontiff. The lesson was unmistakable: There would be no more Regensburg addresses. No more questioning of Islam.

This was no isolated incident. The Church had, in fact, long since made its peace with Islam, abandoning courageous truth-telling for the quiet surrender of diplomacy. Gone were the days of the Church Militant, of saints such as Francis of Assisi preaching Christ to the sultan, or Pope Urban II calling Christendom to rise in defense of the faithful. In their place stood a Church eager to embrace interfaith dialogue, where hard truths were softened or silenced altogether.

And so, the leaders of the Catholic Church continued on their chosen path, ever obliging, ever yielding. I didn't know what might come next, but I was certain of one thing: No pope would ever again risk uttering even a distant echo of a truth that might offend. And those who had once fled the sword of Islam for the arms of the Church? They would find only a door quietly, irrevocably closed.

For converts from Islam, this reality was devastating. Many of us had risked our lives to embrace Christ, only to find that the very Church we had joined seemed reluctant to acknowledge the cost of our conversion. We were left alone. And others, too, paid the price for it.

In 2016, when Fr. Jacques Hamel — an eighty-five-year-old French priest — was slaughtered at the altar by a Muslim during morning Mass in France, the nun who witnessed his murder recalled how the attacker smiled as he slit the priest's throat.

Five days later, a journalist asked Pope Francis whether Fr. Hamel had been killed in the name of Islam. The pope responded: "I don't like to speak of Islamic violence because, every day when I browse the newspapers, I see violence here in Italy.... This man murders his girlfriend, another kills his mother-in-law ... and these are baptized Catholics! There are violent Catholics! If I speak of Islamic violence, I must also speak of Catholic violence."

I was stunned. How could the Holy Father draw a moral equivalence between domestic crimes and jihad? If a Catholic commits murder, it is a grave sin, a direct violation of Christ's teachings. But if a Muslim slaughters a priest while shouting *Allahu Akbar*, he is following the explicit instructions of Muhammed, who commanded jihad against Christians and Jews in sura 9:29 of the Koran.

Jesus never preached violence. Muhammed did.

So, if one insists that violence has "nothing to do with Islam," then one must also argue that Muhammed has nothing to do with Islam.

It wasn't just Pope Francis. Even Pope Benedict XVI, one of the greatest theological minds of our time, fell into this trap, perhaps because he had learned a lesson from his Regensburg address. In *Christianity and the Crisis of Cultures*, he wrote: "Even terrorism is ultimately based on this modality of man's 'self-authorization,' not the teachings of the Qur'an."[8]

It was a baffling claim. How could a scholar as brilliant as Joseph Ratzinger fail to recognize the clear and violent statements in Muhammed's own words, where he claimed: "I have been made victorious with terror!" (Bukhari, Hadith 2977)?

And yet, this was the reality: The very leaders of the Church, whom one might expect would be the strongest defenders of truth, had chosen instead to relativize it. Either out of ignorance or for the sake of survival, they embrace the idea of a peaceful Islam, which is a comforting Western illusion, born not out of scholarship but wishful thinking. People in the West need to recognize that Muslims are not Islam. When we speak of Islam, we are not referring to the practices of Muslims — who can be sincere individuals — but to the teachings of Muhammed. Yet, time and again, we are reassured that Islam itself is a religion of peace and that the Koran, like the Bible, contains both peaceful and violent passages — as if this alone resolves the question of its true nature. It does not. Islamic jurisprudence resolved this matter long ago through *naskh*, or abrogation. Accepted by all four Sunni schools (which represent the majority of Muslims in the world), this doctrine asserts that Muhammed's later revelations supersede his earlier ones.

---

[8] Joseph Cardinal Ratzinger (Pope Benedict XVI), *Christianity and the Crisis of Cultures*, trans. Brian McNeil (Ignatius Press, 2006), 42.

Since the Koran is not written chronologically, how do we determine which came later? By geography. The verses from Muhammed's time in Mecca, when he was a solitary preacher striving for converts, are the earliest. These verses emphasize tolerance and coexistence, as he had little choice but to take this approach.

After his message was rejected by the inhabitants of Mecca and by the Jews and Christians, Muhammed gained significant influence in Medina when local tribes granted him military power. By that point, he was no longer a man seeking followers but a leader with an army to unleash. His message shifted from persuasion to conquest. The calls for understanding vanished and were replaced by calls for the sword.

Sura 9 of the Koran — *At-Tawbah* — was revealed in Medina, and it stands apart from every other chapter in one key respect: It does not begin with the traditional phrase invoking God's mercy. That omission is not accidental. It signals a shift in tone, and in purpose.

The chapter begins with a blunt announcement: "This is a disavowal from Allah and His Messenger to those with whom you made treaties among the polytheists" (sura 9:1). In other words, the agreements once made with non-Muslims are now null and void. The time for diplomacy had ended.

Soon after comes one of the most quoted and controversial verses in the Koran: "Kill the unbelievers wherever you find them" (sura 9:5). It is not vague. It is not metaphorical. It is a call to arms.

The rest of the chapter continues in that same stark tone. Nonbelievers are to be fought. Jews and Christians are to be tolerated only if they pay the *jizya* tax — a symbol of their submission. And Islam is no longer to simply exist among other faiths. It is to prevail over them.

These are not vague allegories, but direct commands issued when Muhammed was at the height of his power.

Some Islamic scholars have debated whether these orders were meant for their time alone or were eternal decrees, but those who suggested the former were dismissed as "heretical" on the grounds that the last chapter of the Koran contained Muhammed's final orders to his men.

To pretend otherwise is not only naive; it is dangerous. These are the verses that ISIS and al-Qaeda, Hamas, and their like do not misinterpret but take to their logical conclusion. The doctrine of abrogation is not a relic of medieval theology; it remains fundamental to the ideology of jihad. It is what students learn in the thousands of madrassas in Pakistan and all around the world. In fact, the very meaning of the word Islam is "submission" — not "peace," as is so often stated by Muslims in the West. And the meaning of Muslim is "one who submits."

For more than a thousand years, this principle of jihad has shaped the fate of civilizations. The Middle East, North Africa, Anatolia — once heartlands of Christianity — were inexorably transformed. The Byzantine Empire, the stronghold of Orthodox Christianity, was crushed beneath the weight of Muslim armies. Turkey, where St. Paul once walked and where believers were first called Christians, bears hardly a trace of its past. Egypt, the land where the Holy Family once found refuge, has become a place where Christians live in fear. These were not gradual cultural shifts because of a decline in births. They were the result of conquests and relentless waves of persecution. To pretend otherwise is to erase history.

Islam divides the world into two realms: Dar al-Islam — the house of Islam, where Islamic rule prevails — and Dar al-Harb — the house of war, where Islam has yet to reign. The implications are clear, and their consequences have played out over the centuries. Egypt was once entirely Coptic Christian; today, the Copts are an embattled minority. Syria, once a thriving Christian land, has seen its ancient communities dwindle to near extinction. These are not accidents of time. They are the results of a system designed to subjugate. Once a land is Islamized, it must remain so. And lands that are not yet Islamized must, in time, be brought into submission.

While the Christian West has drifted toward secularism, shedding its faith like an unfashionable garment, Islam remains what it has always been: a religion bound to a political and military framework. There is no concept of a "post-Islamic" nation. To leave the faith is to invite hostility, exile, or worse.

Traditional Islam is a religion of strategy, one that governs its expansion with the same approach Muhammed himself took. When in a position of weakness, it preaches peace. When in power, it demands submission.

Modern Muslims often say that Muhammed fought only in self-defense. Many hold this belief with sincere conviction. Yet few have studied their own texts deeply enough to challenge it. Instead, their understanding is shaped by an unconscious blending of Islam with the values of modern pluralism. But this is not the Islam of Muhammed.

In surah 33:21, the Koran explicitly instructs that the life of Muhammed be regarded as the ultimate example for all Muslims. His actions, whether peaceful or violent, are divinely authorized and form the basis for all interpretations. His words leave no room for ambiguity: "Fight those who do not believe in Allah and the Last Day, nor comply with what Allah and His Messenger have forbidden, nor embrace the religion of truth from among those who were given the Scripture (Jews and Christians), until they pay the tax (for being non-Muslims), willingly submitting, fully humbled."

Note that this verse does *not* command Muslims to fight Christians and Jews in self-defense or in response to an attack, but solely because they do not believe in Allah.

Jihad is not a distortion of Islam; it is one of its foundations. When modern Muslims insist that terrorists are not real Muslims, they ignore the fact that the terrorists are in reality following Muhammed more faithfully.

Growing up in Dhadar, where I had no links to any terrorists, I bore hatred for non-Muslims, not because of al-Qaeda or ISIS, but because it was the message of the Prophet, preached from the minarets of the mosques of Pakistan. If anything, it is modern Muslims who are reinventing Muhammed's words, because many of them, just like Pope Francis and others, have never even bothered reading the Koran and Hadith themselves. So, all they offer the public are empty clichés about the harmony of world religions, while Muhammed himself insists: "I have been commanded to fight against people till they testify that there is no god but Allah, that Muhammed is the messenger of Allah" (Sahih Muslim, bk. 1, Hadith 36). This is the core ideology that drives Muslim terrorists in Europe to attack innocent civilians and stab them to death, and the sword of Islam will not rest until the entire world submits. For those who do resist, the reality is brutally harsh: flee or die. Ayaan Hirsi Ali and Salman Rushdie were among the first to be driven out of Europe, forced to abandon the continent as radical Islam began to take root. I, too, have followed their path, seeking refuge in the one land that still promised safety — America, the land of second chances.

16

A Warning to the West

WHEN THE PLANE touched down on American soil, I was overwhelmed by a strange mix of relief and dread. America: the land of possibilities, where people could reinvent themselves, where freedoms were promised, and where the past could be left behind. But as I stepped off the plane, I felt an immediate difference. The air was thick with unfamiliarity, and the promises of freedom felt distant, almost like the ideals I had once clung to when I arrived in Europe.

"Hey, how are you?" the officer asked, breaking my thoughts. I could still hear my Austrian friend's voice echoing in my mind: "When they see you were born in Pakistan, they won't even let you in. Remember 9/11? You Pakistanis hid Osama Bin Laden, and Americans won't forget that," my Austrian friend joked, though there was a trace of anti-Americanism in her words.

But in that moment, I didn't face the hostility I had expected. The immigration officer glanced at my passport, then looked up at me, his eyes widening. "Pakistan?" he asked. He called over his colleague, pointing at him. "He's from Pakistan too." They had a brief conversation with me and meanwhile, the people behind in the line grew impatient. "Look straight into the camera," the officer instructed. I did, instinctively posing, just as I had for my photo shoots in Vienna. He chuckled.

As I stepped out of the terminal, the city lights washed over me. I had come here with the hope of a new life and a new identity. But deep down, I couldn't help but wonder: Would I find a place to truly breathe here, or would America, too, eventually become just another cage?

For more than a decade now, I have called the United States my exile.

When I share my experiences of Europe's great unraveling with my fellow Americans and explain why I had to flee, I'm often met with blank stares or polite nods — signals of disbelief rather than understanding. In fact, if there's one thing that unsettles me even more than the persecution I have faced, it's the question that inevitably follows: Is it really that dangerous?

This betrays a striking blindness, not just to the history of Islam but to the reality unfolding around them. In America, it is easy — comfortable, even — to believe that Europe's struggles with Islamic extremism are overstated. From across the Atlantic, one can afford to assume that these attacks are rare, the fears exaggerated, and the warnings little more than right-wing scaremongering. But that assumption requires a deliberate act of blindness.

The reality is far grimmer. Knife attacks, especially against critics, car-rammings, bomb plots, and outright massacres have become a part of daily life in Europe, with authorities either unable or unwilling to halt the rising tide. In Germany alone, police recorded nearly nine thousand knife attacks in 2023; that is twenty-four every single day. Twenty-four times a day, someone is stabbed in what was once one of the safest nations on earth. And yet, officials assure the public that everything is under control, that there is no pattern, and that anyone noticing one is simply "fearmongering." You are not supposed to notice what you see with your own eyes.

The following is not a historical record, nor a tally of long-forgotten tragedies. It is a snapshot, as I write, of the last several months — an incomplete list of events that took place in the short span in which I wrote this book. Those who insist that "it isn't that bad" might want to ask themselves: If this isn't a crisis, what exactly would one look like?

May 31, 2024 – Mannheim, Germany: German Islam critic Michael Stürzenberger was stabbed in a knife attack that left six people injured, including a young police officer who later died. The attacker, twenty-five-year-old Afghan national Sulaiman Ataee, was shot by police.

June 15, 2024 – Wolmirstedt, Germany: An Afghan man fatally stabbed one person before running into an UEFA Euro 2024 watch party, where he injured three others.

July 29, 2024 – Southport, England: A seventeen-year-old migrant attacked children at a dance studio, killing two girls on the scene and critically injuring ten others. A third girl died the following day. Initially, police denied links to Islamic terrorism, but later reports confirmed that the suspect had been charged with possessing an al-Qaeda training manual.

August 8, 2024 – Austria: A Taylor Swift concert was abruptly canceled after authorities discovered a plot by three men with ties to ISIS, who intended to carry out a mass-casualty attack targeting "tens of thousands" of fans.

August 15, 2024 – Galway, Ireland: A Catholic priest was stabbed by a sixteen-year-old radicalized by jihadist propaganda. Investigations revealed the attacker had been sharing content from an Islamic terror group linked to al-Qaeda and ISIS.

August 23, 2024 – Solingen, Germany: A twenty-six-year-old Muslim migrant attacked festivalgoers, killing three Germans. Witnesses and police confirmed he deliberately targeted the throats and necks of victims, following ISIS-style execution methods. ISIS later claimed responsibility.

November 6–7, 2024 – Amsterdam, Netherlands: Israeli soccer fans were brutally attacked by migrant mobs before a match, incited by a "Jew Hunt" campaign circulating on social media. In response, Israel dispatched rescue planes for its citizens.

December 20, 2024 – Magdeburg, Germany: A Saudi migrant drove a vehicle into a crowded Christmas market, killing six people, including a nine-year-old child, and injuring three hundred others.

January 7, 2025 – Vienna, Austria: A Syrian migrant, accused of sexually abusing a twelve-year-old Austrian girl, was acquitted of rape charges. He then gave the victim's lawyer 100 euros. The victim's mother was devastated by the verdict, crying over the perceived injustice and her daughter's humiliation.

January 29, 2025 – Sweden: Iraqi critic of Islam Salwan Momika, who had been living in hiding, was shot and killed in his apartment. Sweden declared that foreign powers were involved in his execution.

February 13, 2025 – Munich, Germany: A twenty-four-year-old Afghan asylum seeker drove into a crowd of 1,500 labor protesters, injuring or killing thirty-six people. Among the dead were a mother and her two-year-old child. The suspect shouted "Allahu Akbar" upon arrest.

February 15, 2025 – Villach, Austria: A twenty-three-year-old Syrian refugee killed a fourteen-year-old Austrian teen and wounded five others in an attack motivated by jihadist ideology.

February 21, 2025 – Berlin, Germany: A nineteen-year-old Muslim terrorist launched an attack at the Holocaust Memorial, stabbing a Spanish tourist whom he mistook for a Jew.

February 22, 2025 – Alsace, France: A thirty-seven-year-old Algerian man killed an innocent Portuguese man while shouting "Allahu Akbar."

February 23, 2025 – Aschaffenburg, Germany: A twenty-eight-year-old Afghan migrant targeted a group of small children, slitting the throat of a two-year-old as a German man tried in vain to protect them.

March 20, 2025 – Germany: Due to rising fears of terror attacks, authorities canceled all public spring festivals nationwide.

Despite this, the troubles of the Old World seem like distant echoes, reverberations from across the Atlantic, barely worth a second thought. America, vast and proud, believes itself immune, shielded by oceans and by its own unique history.

Many Americans see their immigration struggles through a different lens. Here, immigrants have been able to cross the border illegally, but when they stay, they assimilate — if not in the first generation, then surely in the second. It has been the American story for centuries: the Irish, the Italians, and the Eastern Europeans who arrived in waves and became, in time, indistinguishable from those whose ancestors had been here from the beginning. Americans, in their optimism, assume the same will happen with the Muslim immigrants who settle on their shores.

But Islam is different. It is not merely a religion; it is a way of life, a totalizing force that does not bend to the cultures it encounters. It absorbs, it overtakes, but it does not assimilate. Authentic Islam considers itself in a perpetual struggle with all lands that do not submit to the law of the Prophet. In times of weakness, it may wear a smile, may adapt outwardly to the norms of the host society. But at its core, it remains unchanged.

I once met a nurse, a young Pakistani woman in a bustling American city. She seemed entirely Western — her accent flawless, her demeanor modern, her attire indistinguishable from that of any other young professional. And yet, one day, she confided in me that her father had chosen a husband for her back in Pakistan. She spoke with quiet resignation: "I can refuse and lose my parents … or I can just marry him." Even in America, even in the land of the free, she was trapped. And no one around her even noticed.

That is why I bristle when I see the same naivete here that I once encountered in Europe. I have stepped into Catholic churches in America only to find prayer mats and copies of the Koran placed reverently before the tabernacle by well-meaning priests. The same blindness that allowed Europe to slip into crisis is taking root here, ushered in with words like "tolerance" and "dialogue," all while the problems of the Old World creep silently onto American soil. Walk through certain neighborhoods in New York and you will find Islamic bookshops lined with jihadi literature, the seeds of a storm waiting to take root. By 2050, the Muslim population in America is expected to more than double to 8.1 million, surpassing the number of Jews and making Muslims the second-largest religious group in the country.

This growth is primarily fueled by significantly higher birth rates among Muslim families and ongoing immigration. Muslims tend to have younger populations and larger families, which contributes to their rapid expansion. According to a Pew Research study, Islam will be the only major religion growing at a pace faster than the world's population: "Muslims will grow more than twice as fast as the overall world population between 2015 and 2060, and, in the second half of this century, will likely surpass Christianity as the world's largest religious group."[9]

---

9   Michael Lipka and Conrad Hackett, "Why Muslims Are the World's Fastest-Growing Religious Group," Pew Research Center, April 6, 2017, https://www.pewresearch.org/short-reads/2017/04/06/why-muslims-are-the-worlds-fastest-growing-religious-group/.

While Western birth rates continue to decline, Muslims are having children in greater numbers. And unlike Christianity, which has seen mass departures and quiet defections, Islam retains its followers with a tenacity that is both remarkable and unsettling. Few dare to leave, not just out of conviction but out of fear of reprisal. But Islam's power is not merely numerical — it lies in its structure.

While the West, in its relentless pursuit of material progress, has spent decades dismantling the very foundations of the family, Islam has built its culture around an unshakable core. The extended family and the deep-rooted community ties are pillars that remain unbroken, while the West continues to raise generation after generation in the cold, lonely embrace of individualism and isolation.

I have seen firsthand what happens to children in a culture that prioritizes career, comfort, and convenience, where success is more important than relationships. In America, the cycle begins early. Mothers, out of necessity or ambition, leave their newborns to return to work within six weeks. The child is passed from one institution to another — daycare, preschool, kindergarten, aftercare. Even in Catholic schools, little children in lower grades spend almost thirty to forty hours a week away from their family.

By contrast, in Pakistan and much of the Muslim world, children grow up surrounded by family — mothers, grandparents, cousins, aunts, and uncles — offering them a strong foundation of emotional security that helps them cope with difficulties later in life. Meanwhile, in the West, children are increasingly raised by their peers rather than their families. Friendships, not familial bonds, often become the primary source of influence and emotional support. This shift marks a profound departure from traditional Christian family structures, where the family played a central role in raising and guiding children.

And what does this create? A generation that is restless, anxious, and narcissistic. Starved for love and belonging, unwilling to sacrifice but always looking for the love that they didn't receive as children. Then we wonder why our elderly die alone in nursing homes, why our children rebel without cause, why our societies feel more fragile than ever before.

I do not say this to shame parents. I say it to draw attention to a contrast that the West refuses to acknowledge. While we systematically dismantle our foundations — discarding family as outdated, treating faith as an accessory, and embracing a hollow, consumerist existence — Islam embraces the family ever more fiercely. It strengthens the very structures we are abandoning. And in doing so, it grows stronger while we grow weaker.

The West stands at a crossroads. Will it reclaim what it has lost? Or will it continue its slow, unthinking surrender? Only time will tell. But time is running out.

There is a rising tide sweeping across America, an undercurrent so subtle that few have noticed it yet. Islamization is taking root, its growth quiet yet undeniable, while American leaders — blinded by their own idealism — fall for its false promises, just as their European counterparts once did. Consider, for instance, George W. Bush, who, in the aftermath of 9/11, stood before the world and insisted that Islam was "a religion of peace." Meanwhile, in the streets of Kabul, voices rose in unison, chanting "Death to America!" The ignorance is staggering. Christianity is scrutinized for every transgression of its clergy, yet Islam is shielded from critique — even when its followers fly planes into American landmarks. And the presidents who followed Bush fared no better. At the United Nations General Assembly in 2012, Barack Obama proclaimed, "The future must not belong to those who slander the prophet of Islam."

Meanwhile, terrorists already walk among us, waiting for the right hour to strike — to fulfill the commands of their prophet in a relentless jihad against the infidel. The atrocities committed against Christians in Nigeria, where thirteen Christians are killed every day, the bloodshed of October 7, 2023 — these are not distant tragedies; they are a foretaste of what may yet unfold on American soil. For the foot soldiers of jihad, no treaty, no concession, no plea for peace will ever suffice while the caliphate remains unfulfilled. Their allegiance is not to nations or leaders but to the immutable words of Muhammed: "Fight against those who do not believe in Allah."

America has already revealed its vulnerability. When thousands of people poured into the streets to rejoice over murdered Jewish babies and raped women after the October 7 jihad against Israel, the reality became undeniable. These were not foreign radicals cheering from a distant land — they were here, in the heart of our cities, on the campuses of our universities, emboldened and unafraid. The same voices chanting in celebration today will be the ones wielding knives against the innocent tomorrow. And yet, many refuse to see the storm gathering on the horizon.

When I speak of these things among my fellow Christians, I am met with indifference. These people, kindhearted and serious, brush aside my concerns with patient smiles, as though I were recounting the superstitions of a bygone age. I have pleaded with priests, bishops, and religious sisters — well-intentioned and fervent in prayer — but their understanding of Islam remains clouded by the language of ecumenical diplomacy and, understandably, of fear. At the same time, in my daily life, there are those who equate their minor inconveniences with the unspeakable trials of those suffering under the yoke of religious oppression.

They speak of their daily burdens as though they were crosses of martyrdom. The ordinary trials of life — raising children, navigating political discourse — are lamented as if they were tribulations of biblical proportion. I see it everywhere. A priest will stand at the pulpit, his voice rich with reverence, and proclaim Jesus' words: "Greater love has no one than this, that someone lay down his life for his friends" (John 15:13, ESV). But then, with a benign smile, he assures his congregation: "Dear parishioners, by being good mothers and fathers, you are laying down your lives."

The question must be raised: Since when did changing diapers and packing school lunches become acts of martyrdom, Father? Parenthood is selfless, yes — but let us not blur the lines between duty and the sacrifice of one's life. Let us not diminish the gravity of suffering persecution by cloaking the mundane in the language of the heroic.

It is one of the great ironies of our age that those born into the extraordinary privilege of the West — particularly in America — seem the least aware of it. This is not a condemnation, but an undeniable truth. Unlike many, I have lived both in the Muslim world and in the free societies of the West, and the contrast is staggering. What so many fail to grasp is that the liberties they take for granted are not the default state of human civilization. They are the exception, a fragile miracle in a world where tyranny is the rule.

I know well the struggles of daily life in this nation. But there is a far graver matter at hand, one that too many in the West refuse to see. While we waste our breath on petty grievances, forces far from our sight watch, wait, and strategize. They do not see a civilization engaged in noble self-reflection. They see a civilization weakened by narcissism and self-doubt, paralyzed by guilt, and ripe for conquest.

History has little mercy on those who fail to learn from it. Weakness invites aggression. And nothing signals weakness more clearly than the West's staggering indifference to the suffering of its own. Across the world, Christians are harassed, exiled, and slaughtered. And what response do their brothers and sisters in the West offer? Silence. Is it ignorance? Cowardice? Or the naive belief that such horrors could never reach their own shores?

Complacency is a dangerous illusion. The duty of the fortunate is not to turn away in passive comfort, but to stand, to pray, and to act. If we do not summon the will to defend the persecuted now, we should harbor no illusions: One day, we will be called to answer for our indifference.

Is there anything colder than a Christian who doesn't care about his persecuted brother or sister? This coldness is a result of weak charity. Christianity is not a therapeutic faith of self-love. It is about self-sacrificial love. It requires an openness to loss, pain, and suffering. And yet it is freeing. When we open ourselves to following the will of God, to the selfless service of others, the Holy Spirit blows His breath on the sailboat of our lives, leading us beyond our limitations. And at that point, we are not moving by our power, but by God's. Beyond our limitations, beyond the petty comforts that end at the American border. We are not given our freedom merely to enjoy it. We have a profound responsibility to use it to set Christ free where He is bound in chains.[10]

If you think you have nothing in common with your persecuted brother because he is not American — because you do not know him or his culture — you are saying you have nothing in common with Christ. After all, it is Christ who is renewing His Passion in the persecuted. How can you say you are close to Jesus if you don't feel His pain? I feel this pain every day. My soul seems always active, whether I sleep or walk, whether I sit or stand. I miss my family, but my soul does the hard work of persevering.

Every day I live Christ's words: "If anyone comes to Me and does not hate his father and mother, wife and children, brothers and sisters, yes, and his own life also, he cannot be My disciple" (Luke 14:26, NKJV).

---

[10] Catholics must make an effort to understand the immense challenges Muslims face when they choose to leave Islam, so that they can better support those who take that difficult step. By doing so, we can help ensure that these new converts don't fall back into Islam — a tragic reality, as many Muslim converts end up leaving the Christian faith after five years of practice. This happens because they often lack a supportive community that truly seeks to understand their struggles. What if every parish in America made it a priority to say one Our Father after Holy Mass on Sundays for Christians who are suffering persecution? Our brave brothers and sisters are making the ultimate sacrifice of their lives for Christ. Can we not offer the sacrifice of one prayer in return?

Epilogue

People tell me I am lucky. They smile and say, "Look at this new life you've built. Isn't it wonderful?" They mean well, but they do not understand.

Exile is not freedom. It is not a fresh start. It is a severing. It is being torn from the only home you've ever known, with no way back. I will never walk the streets of Dhadar again, never hear the laughter of my cousins, never belong to the community that once shaped me. I will never stand in the doorways of my neighbors in Austria. My homeland is no longer mine. There were no goodbyes. No last embraces. No final words.

Sometimes, I dream of going back anyway. But then, I am confronted with the stories of girls who tried — who longed for home just as I do — yet never returned. Just recently, I learned of the story of Zara, a young Pakistani woman from the United Kingdom with a story so like my own. One day her mother told her that the whole family was returning to their home country for a family wedding. Zara was so excited: She was looking forward to meeting her cousins after so many years. On the flight over to Pakistan, she spent a long time speaking to the flight attendants, whose ranks it was her dream to join. And once she was back in the ancestral village, she felt even happier: Her parents were so kind to her, buying her fine clothes and treating her as if she were the bride.

Little did Zara know that that was just what they had in mind for her. One morning, just a week before the wedding, Zara's mother and father called her into the room and said that they wanted to discuss a very important matter with her. They informed her that she was to marry her cousin. At first, she could not understand. But when her father repeated the words, she was shocked and went blank. So, this was why everyone had treated her so well! She flatly refused, citing reasons of age, education, and her professional ambitions. All in vain. Her parents informed her that the wedding had already been arranged. Zara sought mercy from her mother; it was refused. She wept all that night.

But she decided to stand up for herself. She knew she could call "someone" and that there was a way out. And so she did. After much struggle and emotional blackmail, she was able to make her way back to the U.K. to put her life back together. It was a difficult time. Her father was furious because of the shame he had to endure. But slowly, slowly, things seemed to get better for Zara. And soon, her family — whose honor had also been deeply wounded — tried to get back in touch with her. First the siblings, then the mother. She would speak to them and go and meet them but would not return home.

Then one day, her mother told her that her father wanted to apologize for having rejected her. Zara decided that it was a meaningful gesture and resolved to forget all the violence and return home. So she did. Everything seemed normal again. Her parents apologized and suggested that they go back to Pakistan again to show family unity and restore their lost honor. She agreed, reluctantly. There had been no renewed discussions about the wedding, but she still had her doubts. The only thing planned, as far as she knew, was a family outing to the mountains. And there, as she was walking along the riverside with her father, he regained his honor. He drowned her. Zara, who wanted to fly high in the sky, ended up in the depths of a roaring river.

When I hear stories like Zara's, my own suffering is renewed. I feel compelled to speak up for Zara and others like her, but then I think of my own family. I don't like to talk about how they treated me — not because I haven't forgiven them, but because I know it would hurt them. Despite everything, I still love them, just as Zara did. I can only imagine the isolation and rejection from the Muslim community that my family must already endure, especially my mother who was already constantly sick.

Every time I feel like I can't continue to hurt them by telling others my own story, the image of the man on the Cross appears before me. He silently looks down at His mother. And I realize how His heart must have torn to see her in pain! Yet, He fulfilled His Father's will. This is what I, too, must do: endure with Christ on the Cross.

I know my suffering was not in vain. It has become a mission, a source of healing and hope for others. This is why I continue to move forward, despite the risks. Recently, someone with ties to Homeland Security warned me that writing a book like this could pose an immeasurable threat to my personal safety. "The same people who persecuted you in Europe now live here, too, and their numbers are growing!" he said. "Your anonymity will be gone if you speak out."

But I believe that being vulnerable for the sake of truth is the cost of courage. With Christ I can bear all threats, humiliations and pain — even the fear of death — for the sake of truth. This is the lesson I learned when the corpse was thrown at my car in Pakistan and I was chased by murderers: There can be no courage without vulnerability. No change without sacrifice. You must expose yourself to harm — and to love — for the sake of Jesus.

People sometimes ask if I consider my life worthless. Nothing could be further from the truth. I want to live — I want to continue my mission. I take precautions, which is why there is security at my lectures. But I also understand that, even with police protection, my calling comes with danger — even in the United States.

Salman Rushdie's case is a stark reminder that no country, not even America, is immune to the forces of jihad. After Ayatollah Khomeini issued a death fatwa against him for *The Satanic Verses*, Rushdie lived relatively peacefully in New York for more than thirty years. Despite the years of safety and distance from those who sought his life, the threat never truly disappeared. In August 2022, at the Chautauqua Institution in western New York, a Muslim radical finally attempted to carry out that death sentence. Rushdie was stabbed multiple times during a lecture, leaving him with permanent damage, including blindness in one eye. This brutal attack serves as a chilling reminder that jihadist ideology is not confined to distant lands — it is here, among us, and it knows no borders. No nation, no matter how strong or free, is immune to the growing threat of Islamic jihad.

When I share these events with my friends, they often tell me that God does not wish this path for me — that I deserve happiness and freedom. But what is true happiness, really? Is it a life of ease, free from struggle, surrounded by crowds and laughter? Is it the fleeting emotional highs we chase by avoiding conflict? If so, then by that definition, my life would surely be considered unhappy. For persecution is nothing more than the conflict that comes when one pursues the truth.

To me, a fulfilled life is one lived with the quiet certainty of purpose. Happiness is not found in comfort but in the courage to walk the path that God has set before me, no matter how difficult. It is knowing I follow the narrow road toward union with Him, seeking only His will — fully aware that His will for His own Son was the Cross.

The fear of discomfort is one of the reasons our Church struggles today. Few are willing to stand first when it matters most, hesitant to disturb others or be disturbed themselves. We chase a false sense of peace, yet true harmony is found when we engage in the conflicts that surround us. The real peacemakers are those who confront evil, who bear the cost of speaking when silence is easier, who serve sacrificially, who fight not with hatred but with conviction.

Do I long for health and joy? Of course. But the path to union with God is paved with sacrifice — a price few are willing to pay. Instead, most choose to remain silent, hoping someone else will suffer in their place. Yet silence is never neutral. Just as cowardice in one person can breed cowardice in another, so too can courage in one person awaken courage in others. One act of bravery can shatter the silence, one voice can stir the sleeping, and one soul willing to stand in the fire can set countless others ablaze with the strength to do the same.

The future will not present itself to us as a gift. It must be fought for despite hardship and losses. But we must not fear. For in our hearts, we carry the voice of Jesus, reminding us: "Blessed are they that suffer persecution for justice's sake: for theirs is the kingdom of heaven" (Matt. 5:10, DRA).

Therefore, I dare to be bold! I wish that I could shout to all the corners of the world that Christ's peace is better than Muhammed's Sharia and jihad. I have recognized a great Truth, and if there is anything worth risking your life for, it is the Truth.

Dear God,

What do I live for?
I do not live for myself,
Nor for my dreams,
Nor to gain any advantage from this fleeting life,
Nor from a consoling friendship

Or a family member.
My body, my soul, my heart, my strength —
All that I am, belongs to You.

If You wish for me to be forgotten,
To fade into the shadows of this world,
Let Your will be done.
If it pleases You more that I speak to the nations,
Let Your will be done.

Do with me as You desire,
But never let me be parted from You.
I live to make You more loved,

To win souls for You,
To endure rejection for Your name,
To give without expecting,
To sow without ever reaping.

And when the depths of exhaustion pull me down,
The Queen of Heaven, with gentle hands, mends my shattered wings —
And I rise again, stronger than before.

And this has been the mystery of my life.
That each time life within me seems to fade,
You always resurrect it anew.
It must have been for this very reason,
That You showed up into my life not through a miracle,
But Your Cross.
That I may share in Your pain without dying.
This is my miracle.

About the Author

Sabatina James is an Austrian-Pakistani author, humanitarian, and founder of *Friends of the Passion*, a nonprofit dedicated to supporting persecuted Christians in Pakistan and Nigeria. A convert from Islam to Catholicism, she has devoted her life to freeing Christian slaves, protecting orphans, and rescuing women and girls from forced marriage and honor-based violence. Her international bestselling books, including the acclaimed *Sharia in Germany*, confront oppression with unflinching truth and compassion, earning her the Gerhard Löwenthal Prize for fearless journalism and the Culture Prize of the International Paulus Society. Named Austria's "Woman of the Year" at the 2014 *Look! Gala* in Vienna, Sabatina continues to inspire through her courage, by confronting radical Islam and tirelessly serving those most afflicted by its violence.

Sophia Institute

Sophia Institute is a nonprofit institution that seeks to nurture the spiritual, moral, and cultural life of souls and to spread the gospel of Christ in conformity with the authentic teachings of the Roman Catholic Church.

Sophia Institute Press fulfills this mission by offering translations, reprints, and new publications that afford readers a rich source of the enduring wisdom of mankind.

Sophia Institute also operates the popular online Catholic resource CatholicExchange.com. *Catholic Exchange* provides world news from a Catholic perspective as well as daily devotionals and articles that will help readers to grow in holiness and live a life consistent with the teachings of the Church.

In 2013, Sophia Institute launched Sophia Institute for Teachers to renew and rebuild Catholic culture through service to Catholic education. With the goal of nurturing the spiritual, moral, and cultural life of souls, and an abiding respect for the role and work of teachers, we strive to provide materials and programs that are at once enlightening to the mind and ennobling to the heart; faithful and complete, as well as useful and practical.

Sophia Institute gratefully recognizes the Solidarity Association for preserving and encouraging the growth of our apostolate over the course of many years. Without their generous and timely support, this book would not be in your hands.

www.SophiaInstitute.com
www.CatholicExchange.com
www.SophiaTeachers.org